Quips, Quotes, and Questions

for ~~Quistians~~

Christians

Quips, Quotes, and Questions for ~~Quistians~~ *Christians*

TOMMY GALLOWAY

XULON PRESS

Xulon Press
2301 Lucien Way #415
Maitland, FL 32751
407.339.4217
www.xulonpress.com

Printed in the United States of America.

ISBN-13: 978-1-5456-2726-6

Table of Contents

Chapter 1) Many Mini Devotions 1

Chapter 2) Christian Life. 31

Chapter 3) Closer to Home 64

Chapter 4) Hope for the Holidays 83

Chapter 5) Encouragement 101

Chapter 6) The Faithfulness of God 133

Chapter 7) Inspirational Incidentals 165

Chapter 8) Following and Leading 197

Chapter 9) Words of Wisdom 231

Chapter 10) Finding Humor in Truth 281

Chapter 11) Religion v. Relationship. 295

Chapter 12) Discipleship. 317

Introduction

Since my teenage years, I have been on a quest. A quest to answer the critical questions asked by Christians. All of these years later, I have discovered that there are no easy answers, but all of the answers are recorded in a Book. Not just any book, the Book of Life that is best known as the Bible. In this magnificent Masterpiece, the Author outlines a "quick" fix for all of life's many maladies.

Hebrews 4:12 tells us this, "For the word of God is *quick*, and powerful, and sharper than any two-edged sword, piercing even to the dividing asunder of soul and spirit, and of the joints and marrow, and is a discerner of the thoughts and intents of the heart."

So, the quick Word of God is the quiver that holds the arrows needed to conquer all of life's anxieties. Both the quality and the quantity of the content are without question, containing the answer to every question. While I am personally not qualified to deal with the many difficulties of life, I have found that something as simple as a quote or a quip can equip you with a ray of hope and get you out of your quandary.

I have spent a few years writing the contents of this book. Words inspire me. Someone once told me that I have a way with words. That is not my motive. Jesus said that He was both the

Way and the Word. So, my desire is for everyone to find the Way through my words, by referencing God's Word.

While I have gleaned from others and read a lot from the pages that others have penned, to the best of my knowledge, all of these quips, quotes, and questions were birthed in my brain. If you read something that I wrote and think that you wrote it, please contact me and I will give you credit; but I probably won't give you any cash.

However, I did quote Jesus verbatim throughout this book. I will certainly make sure that He gets His cut, should I get a lot of cash from the sale of these thoughts.

It is my prayer that this book will become a devotion to help with any emotion. Maybe a quote for someone who wants to quit, or maybe a quip for your quiet time. I hope you laugh. I hope you cry. I hope you will refer it to a friend. At the end of the day and at the end of this book, it is my prayer that I have helped every "Quistian" with an inspiring *Quip, Quote,* or *Question*.

Chapter 1
Many Mini Devotions

If you are a chicken, the fire will fry you.
If you are a Christian, the fire will try you.

I'm sure you think that I love chicken. After all, I am a preacher. And you are correct. As a preacher, when I hear the word *chicken*, I start licking my lips. Chicken, in my opinion, is one of the crowns of God's creatures of creation. I prefer it fried, but I like it baked, grilled, broiled, barbecued, stir-fried, and any other way imaginable.

However, like many other words in the English language, *chicken* has a different meaning for the little boy or girl that is being bullied. When they hear the word *chicken*, they perceive it to be the same as the word *coward*.

Prayerfully, I hope no child will accept that insult from some insecure bully. Instead, maybe it will get him or her to turn in faith to Christ. Because once you meet Christ, there is nothing cowardly about living for Him.

Yes, like the little child being called a *chicken*, we as Christians have to understand that life will bring its share of challenges. There will be times that we will go through the fire.

But I love what Isaiah said in Isaiah 43:2, "When you walk through the fire, THOU SHALT NOT BE BURNED!"

And 1 Peter 1:7 says "that the genuineness of your faith, being much more precious than gold that perishes, though it is tested by fire, may be found to praise, honor, and glory at the revelation of Jesus Christ."

When you put these two verses together, you get this: When you are tried with fire, thou shalt not be burned!

You don't need to be a coward or a chicken when life tries you. You are being tried; you are not being fried!

When Christians are talking to other Christians about problems, the four most famous words of advice are *just pray about it*.

When we use the word *just*, what do we mean? *Just*, like many other words in the English language, has a multiplicity of meanings:

1. Very recently, as in it just happened.
2. Barely, by a little, as in I just made it.
3. The gentle formula for giving permission or granting a request, as in, just do it.

So, when we say *just pray about it*, do any of these meanings apply? I don't think so. We need to grasp what *just* means in scripture. *Just* is the same root word as righteous.

I'll let you finish the research. But with this meaning, when we say *just pray about it*, we are actually saying *righteously pray about it*. If you have a need, just find a righteous person to pray with you.

I know you are thinking the Bible says that there is none righteous, no not one, but that means righteous on our own. God hates self-righteousness as bad as He hates unrighteousness, but He loves the fact that He made us righteous through His blood at Calvary.

There is power in prayer, so no matter what you need, bring it to God in prayer!

James 5:16
The effectual fervent prayer of a righteous man avails much.
Just (righteously) pray about it!

The Grammy Awards were recently presented on television. People were awarded for being the best in their field. I have no idea who won or what they won.

However, it did make me think. All of us have a desire to be the best in our field. My entire adult life, I have been in full-time ministry. As a young preacher, I wanted to be the best in my field. I spent about 11 years on what our denomination called the evangelistic field. I stayed busy and traveled extensively.

But now after pastoring for 29 years, I have lost all desire to be the best in my field. Now, I have a greater desire than ever to be the best in God's field.

He said the field is the world, and He is looking for laborers to work in His field. He longingly said the fields are white and ready for harvest, but the laborers are few. The heartbeat of

God is for people to stop working so hard to make a name for themselves and to make great the name of Jesus.

When Jesus comes back, it won't matter how outstanding you were in your field, but whether or not you were out working in His!

Praise God for Peanut Brittle!

In November, Ann and I were at our local Sam's Club when suddenly we had a GOD moment. There on the Christmas aisle was a big plastic container of peanut brittle. Immediately, flashbacks of my childhood raced through my mind. You see, I was raised Pentecostal. In the Pentecostal Church, we were known for the gifts of the Spirit and the gift of making peanut brittle. I can't tell you how many "patties" of this round, precious, golden delicious treat that I have helped to cook, sell, and eat.

Ann "talked me into" getting a container of this delicious treat at Sam's. As I ate, I thought, *"Whoever made this peanut brittle had to have a Pentecostal background. You can't make this stuff taste so good unless you know about the gifts of the Spirit!"*

Now, I know that my title, **Praise God for Peanut Brittle,** combined with writing how simply seeing this yummy treat at Sam's was a God moment seems far-fetched, but you have to finish reading this story.

I pastor Word of Life Church in Tupelo, Mississippi. We have so many wonderful people that God has given us the honor to pastor. But there is one particular family that God is using incredibly to reach their own family. They came to WOLC with minimal knowledge of God or the Bible. They were not raised in a Christian environment at all.

Now, I have to tell you that my greatest joy of pastoring is seeing new people born again and watching them grow in grace. Not only is this one particular family growing in the Lord, but their love for Him is contagious. To date, I have baptized this local family, as well as quite a few of their kinfolks from Texas and Alabama. Their story is a modern-day Book of Acts phenomenon.

Back to the peanut brittle! Recently, another relative from Texas came to visit this family. The lady in our Church had such a burden for her family member (named Wanda) to give her life to the Lord. Sadly, Wanda got very sick and had to spend a lot of time in the hospital. So, our church member requested information on leading her to the Lord. She wanted to make sure that her Wanda got saved while she was here in Tupelo, especially because Wanda had never been around Church too much in her adult life.

I began to visit Wanda in the hospital, and her family always asked me to pray; so I did at their request. While Wanda wasn't rude to me at all, during each visit, I could tell that she didn't want prayer pushed on her.

Another day, I went to the hospital to see Wanda again. As I walked in, I told her how nice she looked. She immediately said to me that she felt swollen. I jokingly said to her, "I am too, but mine is from peanut brittle."

A big smile came across her face, and she told me as a child she had sold many bags of this candy.

She said, "My mother made this and sold it for the Church that we attended."

I asked, "And what kind of Church was that?"

She chuckled and said, "A Pentecostal Church." Then she told me that she was baptized as a child, and she knew all about the gifts of the Spirit.

Then, we conversed about the Pentecostal preachers in the area where she lived, and we both called names that we recognized.

You should have seen the eyes of the lady in our church. She had no idea that Wanda had any religious background, and now her pastor and her aunt were having a conversation about the Church we were both raised in as children!

Don't tell me that God doesn't use seemingly trivial things to relate His love. The two things I want to say are: Never underestimate the seeds sown into the heart of a child. And truly, God's Word will not return to Him void.

Last Sunday, we had the memorial service for Wanda at our church. As I stood there telling the story of peanut brittle, I also got to tell the story of the private prayer that I had with her as she rededicated her life to the Lord!

Now, I don't know if there will be peanut brittle in heaven at the Marriage Supper of the Lamb, but I do know that God used it on earth to help someone get to Heaven.

Praise God for peanut brittle!

As Abraham walked up the mountain to obey the voice of God, he only heard the sound of his son asking, "Where is the Lamb for a burnt offering?"

Even though Abraham was wondering the same thing, he prophetically announced, "God will provide Himself a Lamb."

This journey would put another notch on Abraham's resume as the Father of the Faithful. But quite frankly, faith wasn't defined yet. Abraham was identifying it as he walked by faith and not by sight.

Sometimes in life, when we don't know the answer, we have to speak from the depths of our heart, from our inner-most relationship with God.

Likewise, Abraham had no clue how it was going to happen. He just knew that God would provide. And provide He did!

I still believe in the gift of prophecy, but in some areas of life, we don't need prophecy; we need simple obedience.

Today on our journey of life, we know that God will provide, but more importantly, we need to know that God has already provided. All we need is the vision to see the provision He has already put in place!

When we understand that truth, we move from the past declaration of God *will provide* to the present proclamation of *God has already provided*.

"Delivery to the following recipients failed permanently."

Recently, I received an email from one of our television viewers requesting a particular sermon. Trying to give her an immediate response, I sent her an email to thank her and let her know that a CD or DVD would be sent to her promptly. In a few moments, I checked my email and had an interesting message. The message read, "Delivery to the following recipients failed permanently."

Not being as computer savvy as some, I was sure that it was an error on my part, so I sent it again. The same message immediately was sent back to me. It turns out that there was an error in her email address that we corrected, and it was not permanent.

As I pondered this "error" message, I couldn't help but wonder how many thousands of people are living their lives with no hope because they have been told that their error was permanent.

Yes, certainly, indeed, without a doubt, we have all made our share of errors. The scripture declares that we have all sinned and come short of the glory of God. There is none righteous, no not one.

But the Bible also declares that the blood of Jesus Christ cleanses us from all sin. If that is correct, and I whole-heartedly believe that it is, then there are no permanent errors.

Two thousand years ago, there was a delivery in Bethlehem. It wasn't an *email*; it was *a Male* that just so happened to be the Son of God, the Lamb of God that would take away the sin of the world. This *delivery* had Jesus delivered to those who would put Him on a cross.

When He hung His head on that Cross and said, "It is finished," people thought that the delivery to all the recipients of this great salvation was a permanent error. However, their definition of *finish* and His were a lot different. His finish meant that His work on earth where He had been delivered thirty-three years earlier was complete. In fact, the third day after His death, He got up from the grave and proved that not even the grave is permanent!

Let me remind all of you today that your errors aren't permanent. Your failures are not final, and they are not fatal; they are forgiven by a faithful Father. God's mercy is mightier than your mistakes. His grace is greater than your grief. Now you too can be delivered from the feeling of a permanent error.

Christian Cannibals

As a person with a very weak stomach, it doesn't take much for me to lose my appetite. But if I had to choose the most nauseating, grotesque thing that I can think of, it would be cannibalism. This absurd atrocity is when humans eat the flesh or organs of another human being. That's a taste that I would never want in my mouth.

But sadly, this is a practice among Christians. (Of course, this is figurative language, not literal.)

The Bible clearly states that we are the body of Christ. There are many members of this body with a multiplicity of functions. Yet, it seems to be the trend now to tear down, berate, and belittle any Christian with which we disagree.

Listen to the words of Paul in Galatians 5:15, "But if ye bite and devour one another, take heed that ye be not consumed one of another."

Wow! According to these words, there is cannibalistic Christianity.

No, I do not agree with everyone's philosophy and certainly have questions about other people's theology. But the Bible clearly states that satan is the accuser of the Christian. Why in the world would we want to work in league with that loser and do his job for him? According to Peter, satan is as a roaring lion seeking whom he may devour. So, it seems like a no-brainer that we should not bite and devour the same people that satan is trying to destroy.

It's possible to stand up for what you believe without biting and devouring those with whom you disagree. But sadly, it is my feeling that we are leaving a bad taste in the mouth of non-believers, due to the bad taste in our own mouths after we devour other believers.

Just like in a natural family, Christians will never all get along all of the time. We will have disagreements, and there will be times of misunderstanding; but we are still the body of Christ. There are right and wrong choices and actions, but if we are not careful, we can be right with a wrong attitude.

Why don't we stop chewing each other out, and choose instead to walk in love? We are clearly commanded to build up the body of Christ and not tear it down. Today, I recommit to walk in love and not be a stumbling block to the thousands that are looking for real Christians in a world truly needing Jesus.

It was an ordinary day, or so he thought. The little lad left home that day with five loaves and two fish to sustain him until he returned home. But little did he know that his day would not be an ordinary day!

Now, we have no way of knowing if the boy stumbled onto an outdoor crusade or if he planned on being there. All we know is that he found himself with thousands of other people listening to a man called Jesus. As people sat for hours, the only distraction occurred when people's stomachs started to growl.

Suddenly, the little boy noticed the men with Jesus began whispering and pointing to him. He had no clue that one of the men had spotted his lunch. And before the lad could overthink the situation, the man came and asked him for his bread and fish. He gave it willingly.

Little did this little lad know, but that day his lunch would launch an extraordinary miracle.

The Teacher, Jesus, took those five loaves and two fish, said a prayer, while all of his disciples became servers. As they began to pass the fish out, the fish started to multiply, and so did the bread. At the end of the meal, up to 15,000 had been fed with the little lunch of this lad. Then, they took up 12 baskets of leftovers!

Today, as you begin your day, be willing to give God your little. And remember, it was just an ordinary day when the little lad's little lunch launched a miracle. Who knows! By the end of the day, your little could be turned into a lot.

More importantly, the little that God has given you can be used to bless others. God is not limited by little. He is only limited by what you won't let Him have. If a little lad's lunch can launch a miracle, there is no limit to what God can do with you!

INN Jesus's name:

I know that already most of you are gasping that I would begin this devotion with a spelling error. I hear you saying, "Can't he even spell a word as simple as IN?"

Yes, I can. However, there is no misspelling.

I love the power of the name of Jesus. The Bible says that whatsoever you do in word or deed to do it all in Jesus's name. That should not be just how we close our prayers, but how we open our day.

However, there is a Bible story that merits our attention. It is found in Luke 10:30-37.

A man was taking a journey from Jerusalem to Jericho when thieves overtook him. Not only did they rob him, but they also stripped him of his clothes and wounded him. He was beaten so severely that he was almost dead.

Certainly, this is a sad story, but the most disturbing part is how religion walked by him with unconcern. A Priest came by and saw his condition but kept walking to Church on the other side of the road. A Levite (church worker) saw him and did the same thing.

But then, a "GOOD SAMARITAN" saw him, had compassion, and came to where he was. The Samaritan used his oil and wine to sustain the injured man, and then the Samaritan put him on his own donkey and brought him to an INN. It was IN the INN that the Samaritan took care of him, even paying the innkeeper to let the injured man stay there until he could heal.

My point is this: People need to hear more than you shouting, "In Jesus's name."

They need you to come to where they are and help them get to an Inn where you can help them heal. It's not all based on what you say, but on the basis of what they see in you. Yes, please pray for them in Jesus's name, but also help them get to a place where they are restored.

There are a whole lot of hurting people that need our help. Let's find them, INN JESUS'S NAME!

Sometimes, we confuse the circumstance with the circumference.

Circumference is:

The enclosing boundary of a curved geometric figure, especially a circle. It's a perimeter, a border, or a boundary.

Circumstance is:

A fact or condition connected with or relevant to an event or action.

The circumstances of life are real and relevant to your surroundings. Due to the circumstances that we face, we can be limited in our interactions with people. We say such phrases as "under the circumstances" or "because of circumstances."

And while such a phrase is true at times, this particular reference to circumstance is not necessarily correct. Truthfully, we often allow our circumstances to put us in a circumference.

We enclose ourselves in our situation, allowing that situation to become a boundary and a limitation to a circle that seemingly is not penetrable. Again, while all of that, the circumference of our circumstance, is factual, it is still incorrect.

Think about it! If you are a Christian and you allow your circumstances to put you in a circumference, you are also putting God there. But God doesn't do well in limited circles since He is an unlimited Savior.

He promised that He would never leave you nor forsake you, so He is with you in your circumstance and within the circumference where you have limited yourself. So, what will you do about it?

There is hope! Even though it may be impossible to change your circumstance, you can change your circumference.

Now, I know that nothing is easy, that's why you can't do it alone. You are limited, but your Lord is not!

Today, He wants you to get out from under the circumstances and get out of that limited circumference. With God, all things are possible! He will circumvent your circumstance if you are tired of the circumference.

Some people are more comfortable with chaos than calm.

In Mark 5, we read that Jesus was on a ship with His disciples. While He slept, a massive storm blew water into their boat. It was a chaotic moment that caused them to wake Jesus. When Jesus got up, He rebuked the wind; then He rebuked His disciples. At His rebuke, the wind stopped, and the Bible says there was a great calm. He asked the disciples, "Why are you so fearful, and have no faith?"

The very next verse says, "And they feared exceedingly." I have met so many people like that. Jesus tries to give them calm, but they still can't get past the chaos.

> Mark 4:39-41 states, "And he arose, and rebuked the wind, and said unto the sea, 'Peace, be still.' And the wind ceased, and there was a great calm. And he said unto them, 'Why are ye so fearful? How is it that ye have no faith?' And they feared exceedingly, and said one to another, 'What manner of man is this, that even the wind and the sea obey him?'"

For the past few mornings as I've had my coffee and devotion, I kept hearing a bird hit the big window overhead. Because this kept occurring nonstop, right above my head, it was a bit frustrating during my "quiet" time. This morning, it happened again, so I got up to investigate this new routine interruption. Much to my surprise, it was a dove.

If you know anything about scripture, you know that a dove represents the Holy Spirit. I'll leave the lesson there, but the Holy Spirit can interrupt my devotion any time He chooses. It's the little signs in life that make me know I can make it. It never hurts to start your day with a dove over your head. Ask Jesus.

> Luke 3:22
> And the Holy Ghost descended in a bodily shape like a dove upon him, and a voice came from heaven, which said, "Thou art my beloved Son; in thee I am well pleased."

Dismembered or Transplanted?

There is no greater joy than being a Christian! And it just so happens that God called me to pastor Christian people. While that is a joy too, this blog is about my role in pastoring people that were Christians before I was their pastor.

Now, in all honesty, the greatest joy a pastor can have is to hear the cry of a newly born baby, a person that was just born again. No matter what age that new believer is, it's great to be there when they take that initial step in becoming a Christian. My preference is to have a full house of those new creatures in Christ and watch them grow from milk to meat.

But, with that said, I'm also honored to get to pastor some people that were born again before I was born the first time. God has graced me with some people that are already mature

Christians and has placed them under my leadership to help the continued cultivation of their faith.

However, living in the South in the Bible Belt, it is quite common for people to go from church to church to church. Wherever has the newest fire, the latest technology, the "coolest" worship leader, or the most casual pastor is where people feel "called" to go.

According to my philosophy, if someone tells me that God is moving them to a new church, I give them my blessing and let them move on. Who am I to argue with God? But many times, it's not God that moves them.

There are a multiplicity of reasons why people leave a church, and one of them is total selfishness, an "all about me" mentality. Then, after leaving, those people often begin to talk to other people like Eve talked to Adam, in order to convince them to taste the palatable, new experience at this other church.

While everyone does have a choice, God's design is for all to be a part of a local church body and get established in the faith. That entails staying in the place that you were planted until GOD transplants you to a new field. Otherwise, if you allow some disgruntled Christian to influence you, they are doing nothing more than dismembering the body.

According to 1 Corinthians 12, we all have our place in the body of Christ. Each one of us has a function that only we can fulfill. So, be careful not to let some eager person tell you that God has you in the wrong position in His body.

As I stated earlier, Word of Life Church has some incredible people that came to us from other Christian ministries. I strongly believe that God transplanted them in our body as a vital organ to help us be the body He ordained.

But on the flip side, we have had some other ministries try to dismember some of our precious people. Once someone has been dismembered from where God has placed them, it can be hazardous. Because once dismemberment happens, there is something "missing." You are not just missing church; the body is missing the part that you are destined to fulfill.

My prayer is that every church would fulfill its God-given role and be a place to see the lost saved, not Christians recycled. In the New Testament church, there is a term called *proselyte*. The Biblical meaning of proselyte is to convert someone from sin to salvation. Sadly, the modern-day church has changed the definition of a proselyte to get someone to stop going to one Christian church and move their membership to another.

Paul is known as the greatest preacher of all time. As you read the many books that he wrote in the New Testament, they permeate with power. But intertwined in his compelling story, you also see a lot of pain. As powerful as he was, Paul was not immune to pain. In fact, he implied over and over that his pain was what charged his power.

While I am a positive preacher and person, I'm a little concerned about this generation. As Christians, we want power, but we want someone else to put up the poles, run the lines, and put up the transformers. All we want to do is flip the switch and have power.

While I love to flip switches and say, "Let there be light," I understand that real power comes from God. I also know, according to the Word of God, that life will not be as powerful if it is pain-free.

I'll let Paul speak for himself and wrap it up with Philippians 3:10:

> "That I may know him, and the power of his resurrection, and the fellowship of his sufferings, being made conformable unto his death."

If you want to experience power, you can expect pain.

If you are in the 2nd grade and need to shave, the school system will probably pass you even though you keep failing.

However, God will never pass you to the next level until you pass the test at the level where you are. If you are tired of the same tests, you need to set a meeting with the Teacher. He will take you to His Textbook and show you the answer.

Remember, He wants you to move on as bad as you do. He designed you to become a teacher, but you are hung up being a student.

While your Christian walk always needs continuing education, you are required to pass the basics!

Hebrews 5:12
In fact, though by this time you ought to be teachers, you need someone to teach you the elementary truths of God's word all over again.

Someone recently gave us a gift certificate to an incredible restaurant. A few nights ago I went to pick up a couple of delicious entrees. Realizing that I had enough left on my gift certificate for a delectable dessert, I obeyed my gut. (Pun intended.) The meal was great, but as we sat eating, the beautifully prepared dessert kept my attention all during dinner.

Finally, when the last crumb was gone, I split the dessert between Ann and myself.

She was first to gag, and then me. Without too much info, she and I turned our head from each other, and yes, since we were at home, we spit it out!

I was not about to swallow 143 calories that tasted like that.

Apparently, even gourmet chefs leave out key ingredients. Something was undoubtedly missing that was important.

Yes, it was a little disappointing, but the way my mind works, I felt a Voice from the depths of my soul scream out. I heard the Lord say, "That's what happens most every Sunday. People come to Church to see the beauty of the Lord and to taste and see that the Lord is good."

Yes, He is beautiful! Yes, He is good! However, as a Minister and as a Christian, my prayer is that our Church services never leave out the KEY INGREDIENTS!

I love all of the new technology, but we also have to have the old Theology: Prayer, Worship, and The Word are the essential ingredients needed for any church service.

Revelation 3:16
So, because you are lukewarm-neither hot nor cold-I am about to spit you out of my mouth.

Jonah didn't just tell God, "NO, I'm not going to Nineveh!" He went overboard, both figuratively and literally. If you haven't read this story lately from the book in his name, the story of Jonah shows the love of God in one of the "deepest" ways possible.

Where the story should have ended is when the good part begins. I'm so thankful that God doesn't just let our failures be the storyline. The depth of the love of God changes everything.

But this morning while contemplating the plot of this story, it seemed that as the storm began to rage, Jonah simply gave up. He told the sailors to throw him overboard. There was no reason for Him to live after such direct disobedience to God. Undoubtedly, he felt so small after such a big failure. But all it took was one whale to change his minnow mentality.

After a three day ride in what we call the belly of a whale, and he called "the belly of hell," Jonah received new life and new hope.

I hope that you will get new hope today too! It's not over. No matter how small and insignificant that you may feel, all it takes is one whale to change your minnow mentality. And the good part is, Jesus used the story of Jonah to talk about His love for you.

Matthew 12:40
For as Jonah was three days and three nights in the belly of a huge fish, so the Son of Man will be three days and three nights in the heart of the earth.

Long before Caleb CLIMBED his mountain, he CLAIMED IT.

Forty years is a long time, but it's not a lifetime. Caleb, like many others, had a promise that took forty years to unfold.

And yes, other people hampered him from getting his promise sooner.

He was one of the spies that Moses sent to view the "promised land." He was a visionary and walked into this land and staked a claim on a particular mountain.

Sadly, of the 12 that went out to spy the land, Caleb and Joshua were the only two with faith that God's promise would come to pass.

They took a vote that was 10-2, and sadly, the majority ruled.

The next 40 years brought a lot of changes and challenges. Most of Caleb's friends died, and he became the "senior citizen" of the group.

But God is faithful. Similarly, whatever you claimed, no matter how long ago, can still be climbed!

It took forty years, but listen to the following words from the mouth of Caleb.

> Joshua 14:10-13
>
> "And now, behold, the Lord has kept me alive, as He said, these forty-five years, ever since the Lord spoke this word to Moses while Israel wandered in the wilderness; and now, here I am this day, eighty-five years old. As yet I am as strong this day as on the day that Moses sent me; just as my strength was then, so now is my strength for war, both for going out and for coming in. Now therefore, give me this mountain of which the Lord spoke in that day; for you heard in that day how the Anakim were there, and that the cities were great and fortified. It may be that the Lord will be with me, and I shall be able to drive them out as

the Lord said."

And Joshua blessed him, and gave Hebron to Caleb the son of Jephunneh as an inheritance.

Hey, it can happen for you too. You can still climb whatever you claimed, no matter who or what hampered you when you claimed it. God's promise has not expired!

While preparing for a recent Bible Study about being a servant that truly SERVES the Lord, I felt a strong conviction about some of the things that are "trending" in Christianity. I reluctantly wrote the following post because this is indeed who I think that God has called me to be.

While speaking at a business luncheon recently, I had a very embarrassing moment. If you don't know me well, you will think that I am promoting myself, but if you do know me well, you will see the sincerity of this post.

God has graciously allowed Word of Life Church to have a television ministry. I am not a TV preacher; I am a preacher that preaches on TV. If you want to ruffle my feathers, call our program a show. Still, God has used this ministry effectively throughout our local region. We have quite a few members that are at WOLC as a result of the program, and I have preached funerals, weddings, and met a lot of people because of this media ministry.

However, the very sincere lady that had invited me to speak introduced me at this luncheon as a celebrity. While I would never embarrass her, that truly embarrassed me. Pastors, Preachers, Worship Leaders, and Christian Singers are not celebrities; we are servants!

There should only be one celebrity in our Churches, and He has nailprints in His hands. And, if you will read about His ministry, He washed other people's stinky feet.

Somehow, Christianity has to return to serving Christ by serving one another. Yes, I know that we are sons and daughters of God. I also know that we are Royalty with the blood of Jesus in our veins. But we are all made of dust, and we have this treasure in an earthly vessel.

Celebrity people say, "I'm a Son, not a servant," but Jesus taught that we are both. While there are some "celebrities" who are Christians, there are no Christian celebrities. God called each of us to be a servant, not a celebrity.

The only thing more awkward for Job than the silence of his friends for seven days was when they wouldn't stop talking for weeks.

When Job's friends heard about his demise, that all went to see him, to stand with him through his battle. But when they saw him, it was total shock and awe. For seven days, no one said a word.

After this period of silence, Job began to talk about his sorrows and to voice the void that his loss had brought. But when he finished speaking, one by one his "friends" that came to stand with him began to berate him. Back and forth they went, and instead of being a healing balm for Job, they became another pain in his neck.

I think this story still carries great relevance today. When we see someone that's having a difficult time, we have to discern not just when to speak but what to say when we speak. The last thing that people need when they are in a dark place is another accuser. Sometimes people need a shoulder, not a sermon.

Job 2:11-13
When Job's three friends, Eliphaz the Temanite, Bildad the Shuhite and Zophar the Naamathite, heard about all the troubles that had come upon him, they set out from their homes and met together by agreement to go and sympathize with him and comfort him. When they saw him from a distance, they could hardly recognize him; they began to weep aloud, and they tore their robes and sprinkled dust on their heads. Then they sat on the ground with him for seven days and seven nights. No one said a word to him, because they saw how great his suffering was.

Job 42:10
And the Lord turned the captivity of Job, when he prayed for his friends: also the Lord gave Job twice as much as he had before.

Don't get so busy watching for a SNAKE in the grass and forget about the SNEAK behind the tree.

Lucifer wasn't a SNAKE in the Garden of Eden; he was a SNEAK. When Eve met him, he was downright mean, but he was in an upright position. The Bible tells us that he had been given beauty when God created him as an angel.

Eve probably wouldn't have talked to a snake, but she had no problem conversing with this "good looking" sneak. He spoke to her from amongst the trees about a tree with fruit of which she was not to partake.

While you can read the story in Genesis 3 for yourself, let me remind you that just because something looks good, it's not always good for you.

Neither Lucifer nor the tree of knowledge of good and evil was intended to entice Eve. Eve was merely flirting with something that she should have left alone. There is never a right time to be at the wrong place, but Eve found herself in the wrong place.

At the end of this temptation, the upright Lucifer that was a sneak received a curse from God and became a snake that had to crawl on his belly.

So, don't get so busy looking for the snake in the grass and ignore the sneak that is trying to tempt you!

By the way, Jesus took care of what happened amongst those trees when He hung ON a tree.

Something is fulfilling about getting something new. New car. New house. New clothes. For the first 24 hours, you drive it, look at it, and try it on. It's new. It's beautiful. It's what you've always wanted. Then, over time, all of these things lose their luster-as the new wears off.

God knows best and knows how we humans are. When the new wears off, we tend not to treat whatever it is the same way as we treated it when it was new. So, on our behalf and for His glory, He never lets the new wear off of mercy. He makes it new every morning! Great is His faithfulness!

I invite you today to look at His mercy, try it on, and live in it. And in the morning when you awake, you will find that it still does not lose its luster.

> Lamentations 3:21-23
> This I recall to my mind, therefore have I hope. It is of the Lord's mercies that we are not consumed because his compassions fail not. They are new every morning: great is thy faithfulness.

God never allows the new to wear off of His mercy. He makes it new every 24 hours.

Yes, I am one of those people that talks to myself. I don't converse with me because I am the most intelligent person I know, but I am the only human that truly understands me.

But more profound than that, talking to myself is scriptural.

Today I will focus on two examples. One person said the right thing to herself, and one said the wrong thing to himself. According to the doctors, one was at the point of death, and the other was at the point of an excellent life. Ironically, what each of them said to themselves reversed the outcome of their lives. The one that was supposed to die-lived, and the one that was supposed to live-died.

The one particular lady had an issue of blood; the man had an issue with money. The lady had been sick for 12 years, and most likely, the man had worked hard for the last 12 years.

But here is the difference in their stories. The lady said to herself, "If I could touch the hem of the garment of Jesus, I know I will be made whole." She did what she said, and it happened just like she said! Jesus stopped and asked, "Who touched me?" He declared to her that from that very moment she was whole.

The man, on the other hand, said to himself, "I will say to my soul…" (Now, be careful when you talk to your soul. That's the part of you that will live forever somewhere.)

Sadly, this man merely left God out of his life and let the issue of money talk him out of God's real plan for his life.

Today, as you talk to yourself, encourage yourself to talk to Jesus. It's literally the difference in life and death.

Matthew 9: 20-22

And, behold, a woman, which was diseased with an issue of blood twelve years, came behind him, and touched the hem of his garment: For she said within herself, If I may but touch his garment, I shall be whole. But Jesus turned him about, and when he saw her, he said, Daughter, be of good comfort; thy faith hath made thee whole. And the woman was made whole from that hour.

Luke 12:16-21

And he spake a parable unto them, saying, The ground of a certain rich man brought forth plentifully: And he thought within himself, saying, What shall I do, because I have no room where to bestow my fruits? And he said, This will I do: I will pull down my barns, and build greater; and there will I bestow all my fruits and my goods. And I will say to my soul, Soul, thou hast much goods laid up for many years; take thine ease, eat, drink, and be merry. But God said unto him, Thou fool, this night thy soul shall be required of thee: then whose shall those things be, which thou hast provided? So is he that layeth up treasure for himself, and is not rich toward God.

As a Pastor, obviously, people often ask me to pray for them. So often they say, "I need the Lord to touch me."

That is indeed a valid request. In His earthly ministry, Jesus touched hundreds of people, and their lives were changed. And now as He listens from Heaven, He still touches people.

But what happens when you feel like Jesus hasn't touched you?

As we just discussed, there is a compelling story in the Bible that addresses that situation. There was a lady that had an issue with her blood for 12 years. Each year she tried doctor after doctor but kept getting worse.

One day, she heard that Jesus was passing by. As she stood in the crowd, no doubt she prayed that He would stop and touch her. But, He didn't. So what do you do when you have a need, and Jesus doesn't touch you?

Well, what she did was talk to herself. She said to herself, "If I could touch the hem of Him, I know I will be made whole."

So, she talked herself into pressing her way through the crowd and touching the hem of Jesus's garment. He stopped immediately and asked, "Who touched my clothes?"

The lady confessed it was her touch, so Jesus said to her, "Daughter, your faith has made you whole."

Interestingly, the results from her touch were the same as everyone else's results when He touched them.

I encourage you today to stop waiting on Jesus to touch you. Through prayer, you can press your way through your problems, and you will be able to touch Him.

My prayer for you is that before this day ends, Jesus will touch you, or you will touch Jesus. Either way, at the end of the day, you will have been touched!

People who fall do not need others to pile on. They need someone to pull up.

In football, after a man is down, you cannot hit him. If you come in late on any given play and "pile on," it's called a late hit. Usually, you will incur a personal foul penalty, and your team will be set back 15 yards.

In real life, I can't tell you how many people I have seen "pile on" when someone was already down. Even though we can't mandate a penalty for that, it does set the body of Christ back.

We would be wise to heed the Word of God and handle the fallen the way the Bible says. There are so many scriptures that let the fallen know they can get back up and start all over. But there are also verses that let me know my responsibility of how to react when someone falls.

One of those verses is Galatians 6:1, which says, "Brothers, if a man be overtaken in a fault, you which are spiritual, restore such an one in the spirit of meekness; considering thyself, lest thou also be tempted."

Chapter 2
Christian Life

E ach Christian needs to be a witness and tell others about Jesus. Christians also need to pray and tell Jesus about others.

> Acts 1:8
> But ye shall receive power, after that the Holy Ghost is come upon you: and ye shall be witnesses unto me both in Jerusalem, and in all Judaea, and in Samaria, and unto the uttermost part of the earth.

> James 5:16
> Confess your faults one to another, and pray one for another, that ye may be healed. The effectual fervent prayer of a righteous man avails much.

As a Christian, you have been subpoenaed to be a *witness*, so quit trying to be the *Judge*.

Matthew 7:1-2
Judge not, that ye be not judged.
For with what judgment ye judge, ye shall be judged:
and with what measure ye mete, it shall be measured
to you again.

It is time to take a stand!
Stand up for Jesus.
Stand by your word.
Stand beside your family.
Stand behind your leader.
Stand for your integrity.
Stand with your country.
Stand in for someone in need.
Stand back from the drama.
Stand out from the crowd.
Stand before God.

Most of life's *lessons* are meant to teach us to *lessen* our reliance on self and to trust in God.

John 3:30
He must increase, but I must decrease.

God is not unwilling to forgive.
Some people are just unwilling to ask.

Matthew 7:7-8
Ask, and it shall be given you; seek, and ye shall find;
knock, and it shall be opened unto you.

For every one that asks receives; and he that seeks finds;
and to him that knocks it shall be opened.

Biting your lip is always better than eating your words.

Job 2:10
But he said to her, "You speak as one of the foolish
women speaks. Shall we indeed accept good from
God, and shall we not accept adversity?" In all this
Job did not sin with his lips.

Whether or not we want to admit it, we are always affected
by the attitudes of people that we are around. Whether it is
family, friends, or co-workers, we are susceptible to whatever
mood they are in. However, you have to learn to not let what
affects you *infect* you. Don't let what's around you get in you.

Hebrews 12:15
Looking diligently lest any man fail of the grace of
God; lest any root of bitterness springing up trouble

you, and thereby many be defiled.

James 3:8-11
But no man can tame the tongue. It is an unruly evil,
full of deadly poison. With it we bless our God and
Father, and with it we curse men, who have been made
in the similitude of God. Out of the same mouth proceed blessing and cursing. My brethren, these things
ought not to be so. Does a spring send forth fresh
water and bitter from the same opening?

Everyone needs a home church, where you have a home
field advantage.

Colossians 1:24
Who now rejoice in my sufferings for you, and fill up
that which is behind of the afflictions of Christ in my
flesh for his body's sake, which is the church.

Galatians 6:2
Bear ye one another's burdens, and so fulfill the law
of Christ.

Sometimes in life when you're called to stand for *what's
right*, you are left standing with *who's left*.

Matthew 19:29
And every one that hath forsaken houses, or brethren, or sisters, or father, or mother, or wife, or children, or lands, for my name's sake, shall receive an hundred-fold, and shall inherit everlasting life.

Some of the Bible is a menu.
You sit down, place your order, and wait for it to arrive.
Other parts of the Bible are a cookbook.
You have to prepare and mix a lot of things to get your hunger satisfied.

Psalm 23:5
You prepare a table before me in the presence of mine enemies: You anoint my head with oil; my cup runs over.

Romans 5:3-5
And not only so, but we glory in tribulations also: knowing that tribulation works patience; And patience, experience; and experience, hope: And hope makes not ashamed; because the love of God is shed abroad in our hearts by the Holy Ghost which is given unto us.

One of my favorite verses is John 4:24.

God is a Spirit and they that worship Him must worship Him in spirit and in truth.

Over the past 40 years, I have emphatically declared that verse. I have emphasized over and over that you can't have Spirit without truth, and you can't have truth without Spirit. I still believe that.

However, before there was a John 4:24, there was a John 1:14.

> And the Word was made flesh, and dwelt among us, (and we beheld His glory, the glory as of the only begotten of the Father,) full of grace and truth.

I have also preached from this verse many times. But I confess, I mostly emphasized the first part. Oh, how I love to quote, "and the Word was made flesh and dwelt among us, and we beheld His glory, the glory of the only begotten of the Father..."

But the next part is equally important. Jesus was full of grace and truth!

In my time of devotion this morning, I felt so compelled to remind us that we can worship all day long, in Spirit and truth, but we have to remember that Jesus came with grace and truth.

Spirit and truth without grace are lacking the New Testament's main ingredient.

Let's not forget about the grace; it's still so amazing!

At some point in your life, you will have a friend like Judas, but at no point in your life should you be that friend.

Zechariah 13:6
And one shall say unto him, What are these wounds in
thine hands? Then he shall answer, Those with which
I was wounded in the house of my friends.

Mathew 26:47-50
And while he yet spake, lo, Judas, one of the twelve,
came, and with him a great multitude with swords
and staves, from the chief priests and elders of the
people. Now he that betrayed him gave them a sign,
saying, Whomsoever I shall kiss, that same is he: hold
him fast. And forthwith he came to Jesus, and said,
Hail, master; and kissed him. And Jesus said unto him,
Friend, wherefore art thou come?

Very few people purposefully inflict pain on others. However,
at some point, others will point a finger in your direction and
blame you for their suffering. Hurting people seem to huddle
under their circumstances and blame all of their aches on others.

If you are the one that wounded someone, either on purpose
or accidentally, chances are you will not be the one that can
spread salve on their wound. All you can do is take responsibility for your part, whether it was intentional or not. At that
point, through His grace, God will put people in their path to
help with the healing process.

Through the power of the cross, they can then join Jesus
and say, "Father, forgive them because they don't know what
they are doing."

It's complicated to be the cure for pain-if you are also the cause of the pain.

Luke 23:34
Then said Jesus, Father, forgive them; for they know not what they do.

The original House of Representatives didn't begin in a state or national capital. Jesus designed for each member of His body to represent what His Kingdom looks like, exemplified in the form of Christianity.

When people see us, they are supposed to see an image of Emmanuel exemplified, God with us. All of us, at times, fail to emulate this high calling.

To keep this duty and calling intact, Paul gives us a clear-cut cure in Romans 12:1.

I beseech you therefore, brethren, by the mercies of God, that ye present your bodies a living sacrifice, holy, acceptable unto God, which is your reason-able service.

Before you can represent the body of Christ, you have to present your body to Christ as a living sacrifice.

Then, you can say with Paul in Galatians 2:20, "I am cruci-fied with Christ: nevertheless I live; yet not I, but Christ liveth in me: and the life which I now live in the flesh I live by the faith of the Son of God, who loved me, and gave himself for me."

The *illumination* of the *Son* in your life will cause the *elimination* of *sin* from your life.

> Isaiah 59:1-2
> Behold, the Lord's hand is not shortened, that it cannot save; neither his ear heavy, that it cannot hear: But your iniquities have separated between you and your God, and your sins have hid his face from you, that he will not hear.

At its core, Christianity was designed to be *sacrificial*, not *superficial*.
#keep it real.

> Matthew 23:15
> Woe unto you, scribes and Pharisees, hypocrites! for you compass sea and land to make one proselyte, and when he is made, ye make him twofold more the child of hell than yourselves.

Doubt is nothing more than faith in reverse. When you believe that what you are praying for won't happen, you are usually right.

There are hundreds of *versions* of the Bible, but there is only one way to have a *conversion*.

> Acts 3:19
> Repent ye therefore, and be converted, that your sins may be blotted out, when the times of refreshing shall come from the presence of the Lord;

What you are willing to *come out of* will determine the *outcome* of your life.

> Deuteronomy 6:23
> And he brought us out from thence, that he might bring us in, to give us the land which he sware unto our fathers.

> 1 Peter 2:9
> But ye are a chosen generation, a royal priesthood, an holy nation, a peculiar people; that ye should show forth the praises of him who hath called you out of darkness into his marvellous light:

Our Christianity cannot be hitched to *hype*.
It has to be hitched to *hope*.

1 Peter 1:3
Blessed be the God and Father of our Lord Jesus Christ, which according to his abundant mercy hath begotten us again unto a lively hope by the resurrection of Jesus Christ from the dead...

My poetic version of Exodus 20:17 is:
Thou shalt not covet thy neighbor's house or your neighbor's spouse.

Exodus 20:17
Thou shalt not covet thy neighbor's house, thou shalt not covet thy neighbor's wife, nor his manservant, nor his maidservant, nor his ox, nor his ass, nor any thing that is thy neighbor's.

Heaven is not on my *bucket* list.
It's on my *pail* list.
Compared to Heaven, everything else *pales* in comparison.

Romans 8:18
For I reckon that the sufferings of this present time are not worthy to be compared with the glory which

shall be revealed in us.

Word of Life Church is where people come *expecting* God to do great things, not a place of *inspecting* people who do bad things.

Only after I produce the *fruit* of the Spirit am I qualified to practice the *gifts* of the Spirit.

> Galatians 5:22-23
> But the fruit of the Spirit is love, joy, peace, longsuf-fering, gentleness, goodness, faith, meekness, temper-ance: against such there is no law.

> 1 Corinthians 14:12
> Even so ye, forasmuch as ye are zealous of spiri-tual gifts, seek that ye may excel to the edifying of the church.

> Galatians 6:1
> Brethren, if a man be overtaken in a fault, ye which are spiritual, restore such an one in the spirit of meekness;

considering thyself, lest thou also be tempted.

To me, this verse is the catalyst of Christianity. When a fault *overtakes* people, they should not be *taken over* by fault finders. They need someone to restore them in the spirit of meekness.

You can fake your *identity*, but you can't fake your *integrity*.

A church is not a place to be *bored* again.
It's a place to be *born* again!

> John 3:3
> Jesus answered and said unto him, Verily, verily, I say unto thee, Except a man be born again, he cannot see the kingdom of God.

> Psalm 100:4
> Enter into his gates with thanksgiving, and into his courts with praise: be thankful unto him, and bless his name.

True Christianity is learning how to be the *light*, without having to be in the *spotlight*.

People aren't looking for the light at the end of the tunnel. They are looking for the light in front of them that should shine from the life of a Christian.

Matthew 5:16
Let your light so shine before men, that they may see your good works, and glorify your Father which is in heaven.

Bringing your *past* into your *present* is a *present* to the enemy.

God throws away your past, while the enemy throws it up in your face.

You can know every verse to "I'll Fly Away," but it's only at the air traffic control tower called Calvary that you are cleared for takeoff.

There comes a time in your life that you have to stop praying for *stuff* and start praying for *strength*. Stuff will all diminish at life's finish line, but the power of Christ will propel you across.

Matthew 6:19-20
Lay not up for yourselves treasures upon earth, where moth and rust doth corrupt, and where thieves break through and steal: But lay up for yourselves treasures in heaven, where neither moth nor rust doth corrupt, and where thieves do not break through nor steal:

I know it seems like a technicality with words, but no one can pray *for* you. People can only pray *with* you.

James 5:16
Confess your faults one to another, and pray one for another, that ye may be healed. The effectual fervent prayer of a righteous man avails much.

Psalms 68:1 says, "Let God arise."

I want to say that you can't stop God from rising if He wants to get up. On that resurrection Sunday morning, nobody had to *let* Him out of the tomb.

But, for us to have victory, we have to let God in. He stands at the door and knocks.

The same goes for forgiveness. Calvary's purpose was the remission of our sins. All He asks of us is true repentance.

Yes, you have to give God *permission* for your sins to have *remission*.

It has been proven that looking directly at the Son will not blind you.

In fact, it's the only thing that will truly cause you to see.

Luke 10:22-23

All things are delivered to me of my Father: and no man knows who the Son is, but the Father; and who the Father is, but the Son, and he to whom the Son will reveal him. And he turned him unto his disciples, and said privately, Blessed are the eyes which see the things that ye see.

Correct Christian balance is when you have more *peace in your heart* than *problems on your mind*.

Jesus taught very clearly that whatever measure you use while dealing with others is the measurement that is used for you. This concept is displayed so clearly in Luke 16, with the story of the rich man and a beggar named Lazarus. Lazarus simply asked for a crumb of bread, a request to which the rich man did not comply. After both died, the Bible says that the rich man went to hell and the beggar went to heaven.

In hell, the rich man looked up and asked for Lazarus to bring him a drop of water. It wasn't that Lazarus would not; it's because he could not. So, even after this life, "how you measure, will be measured to you."

Lazarus wanted a *crumb of bread*. The rich man wanted a *drop of water*.

Often people say that someone did "an act of kindness." While that is notable, as Christians, kindness should never be an act. It's an attribute of our Christian faith. Kindness and Christianity cannot be separated.

> Romans 12:10
> Be kindly affectioned one to another with brotherly love; in honor preferring one another;

> Ephesians 4:32
> And be ye kind one to another, tenderhearted, forgiving one another, even as God for Christ's sake hath forgiven you.

Jesus is not just for the *afterlife;*
He is the *life* we are *after* now.

In heaven, we will not look like what we've been through. We will look like Who we came to.

1 John 3:2
Beloved, now are we the sons of God, and it doth not yet appear what we shall be: but we know that, when he shall appear, we shall be like him; for we shall see him as he is.

A church that is Bible-based allows people to come as they are but not leave as they were.

People that are ready for the rapture will make a *clean* getaway.
Are you washed clean by His blood?

2 Peter 3:10
But the day of the Lord will come as a thief in the night; in the which the heavens shall pass away with a great noise, and the elements shall melt with fervent heat, the earth also and the works that are therein shall be burned up.

Christianity is not about *what* you are called.
It's about *Who* you called on.

Christianity is not a *conversation* about Christ.
It is a *conversion* to Christ.

It's okay to *disagree* with a political party, but it's not okay to *disrespect* the people in authority.

> 1 Timothy 2:11-2
> I exhort therefore, that, first of all, supplications, prayers, intercessions, and giving of thanks, be made for all men; For kings, and for all that are in authority; that we may lead a quiet and peaceable life in all godliness and honesty.

Many people love to share your *testimony*, but few were there to share your *test*.

Some people love to name drop the name brand of the items that they buy. But at the end of the day, it doesn't matter if you have Levi jeans, a Louis Vuitton purse, or find your style at Gap, Gucci, or Goodwill. It doesn't matter if you wear Chaps or Chanel or get your bling at Charming Charlie. It makes no difference if your watch is a Timex or a Rolex. Whether you shop at Target, Walmart, Dollar Tree, or Neiman Marcus, that's not the most important name. You don't have to have a name brand, but you do have to have a brand new name.

Revelation 3:12

Him that overcomes will I make a pillar in the temple of my God, and he shall go no more out: and I will write upon him the name of my God, and the name of the city of my God, which is new Jerusalem, which cometh down out of heaven from my God: and I will write upon him my new name.

It's okay to have gray areas on the top of your head, but it's not okay to have gray areas inside of your head.

Some people can't *find* a Church because they don't want to help *fund* a Church.

My new motto for Word of Life Church is as follows:

You won't find a church that has more fun or that takes Jesus so seriously.

When you become a new Christian, you do not have a limited warranty. It's not a three-year or 36,000-mile warranty, and it's not bumper to bumper. It is head to toe.

I was saved when I was 9 and started preaching when I was 16. In the physical, I've driven and flown an estimated two million miles, mostly to proclaim the newness that people can find in Christ.

At 59, I can testify that God still makes His mercy new every morning. Yet, it's up to me to refuel with His presence. His Holy Spirit is compared to oil, so I get frequent oil changes that the Bible calls times of refreshing. But amazingly, I never have to retire. When I'm tired, I just come unto Jesus and rest. He has a rest area just for that.

If you are ready to trade your old life for a new, I know it sounds too good to be true, but it's absolutely free. Jesus paid for it at Calvary. His warranty not only covers you in this life, but it comes with an everlasting lifetime warranty! I'm not just His salesman; I am another satisfied customer.

The criteria for mature Christianity is the ability to be *childlike* without being *childish*.

Matthew 18:3
And said, Verily I say unto you, Except ye be converted, and become as little children, ye shall not enter into the kingdom of heaven.

1 Corinthians 13:11
When I was a child, I spake as a child, I understood as a child, I thought as a child: but when I became a man, I put away childish things.

The Church is a body, not a building.
You go to the building, but you are the church.

Man *crafts* the church *building*, but God *grafts* the church *body*.

> Romans 11:17
> And if some of the branches be broken off, and thou, being a wild olive tree, wert graffed in among them, and with them partakest of the root and fatness of the olive tree;

The church is a place to get together with others who haven't got it together. But, when you get together and worship together, your chances of getting it together increase immensely.

For Adam and Eve, it was a piece of fruit.
For the man in Luke, it was a piece of property.
For Judas, it was thirty pieces of silver.
Don't allow a *piece* of anything to take your *peace* of mind.

At church, the offering is not an *intermission*.
It is a chance to *enter a mission*.

In one of the lowest moments of his life, David longed to disappear. There are times in life that we can all relate to that sentiment. However, one day it will be a reality. When Christ *appears*, we will *disappear*.

> Psalm 55:6
> And I said, Oh that I had wings like a dove! for then would I fly away, and be at rest.

> Titus 2:13
> Looking for that blessed hope, and the glorious appearing of the great God and our Savior Jesus Christ.

The last time I took a poll of Word of Life members, we discovered that our congregation is made up of 19 different denominational backgrounds and other sinners. Even though there is only one kind of Christian, we often reference different denominations as a certain "kind" of a church. I'm not too hung up on the kind of Christian church you attend, but I'm absolutely hung up on if you are a kind Christian.

1 Corinthians 13 says it well. You can speak in tongues and move mountains, but without love, it is all null and void.

Love is patient,

Love is KIND...

Let's put kindness back into our Christianity!

The Holy Spirit is more than a *feeling*; it is a *filling*.

> Ephesians 5:18
> And be not drunk with wine, wherein is excess; but
> be filled with the Spirit;

No matter how hard you try, you will never find the missing *pieces* of your life until you discover the missing *peace* in your life. Try Jesus; He is the Prince of Peace, and also the perfector of peace.

> Isaiah 9:6
> For unto us a child is born, unto us a son is given:
> and the government shall be upon his shoulder: and
> his name shall be called Wonderful, Counsellor,
> The mighty God, The everlasting Father, The
> Prince of Peace.

> Isaiah 26:3
> Thou wilt keep him in perfect peace, whose mind is
> stayed on thee: because he trusts in thee.

Jesus is not *a* way of life. He is *the way, the truth, and the life.*

Just because you sinned doesn't make you a devil, and just because you are good doesn't make you godly.

Today has been a three-tower day. This morning while running, I ran by two towers. I ran by the cellular tower where I get my signal to talk to others. Then, I ran by the water tower that supplies water to my family. But early this morning before I ran by those two towers, I ran into a Strong Tower. Before I talked to others from the cellular tower and enjoyed the water from the water tower, I found safety in talking to the Lord and being washed by the water of His Word. If you can only have one tower today, please choose the Strong Tower!

> Proverbs 18:10
> The name of the LORD is a Strong Tower: the righteous runs into it, and is safe.

Life insurance is good.
Life assurance is better.
Do you have everlasting life assurance?

Jesus began His ministry in the wilderness with hunger and ended it on the cross with thirst. He wanted to relate to all of us hungry and thirsty souls.

> Luke 4: 1-2
> And Jesus being full of the Holy Ghost returned from Jordan, and was led by the Spirit into the wilderness, being forty days tempted of the devil. And in those

days he did eat nothing: and when they were ended, he afterward hungered.

John 19:28
After this, Jesus knowing that all things were now accomplished, that the scripture might be fulfilled, saith, I thirst.

Matthew 5:6
Blessed are they which do hunger and thirst after righteousness: for they shall be filled.

Forgiveness: What is *admitted* by man and *remitted* by God.

1 John 1:9
If we confess our sins, he is faithful and just to forgive us our sins, and to cleanse us from all unrighteousness.

Every Christian has to have their personal mission statement.

Remission of sin.

Submission to the Holy Spirit.

Commission to spread the Good News.

Acts 2:38
Then Peter said unto them, Repent, and be baptized every one of you in the name of Jesus Christ for the

remission of sins, and ye shall receive the gift of the Holy Ghost.

James 4:7
Submit yourselves therefore to God. Resist the devil, and he will flee from you.

Matthew 28:19
Go ye therefore, and teach all nations, baptizing them in the name of the Father, and of the Son, and of the Holy Ghost:

It's not the sign in *front* of the Church that identifies who you are in Christ.

It's the signs *behind* the believer.

Mark 16:15-18
And he said unto them, Go ye into all the world, and preach the gospel to every creature. He that believes and is baptized shall be saved; but he that believes not shall be damned. And these signs shall follow them that believe; In my name shall they cast out devils; they shall speak with new tongues; They shall take up serpents; and if they drink any deadly thing, it shall not hurt them; they shall lay hands on the sick, and they shall recover.

Taking a *seat* at church helps you to take a *stand* in the world.

Hebrews 10:25
Not forsaking the assembling of ourselves together,
as the manner of some is; but exhorting one another:
and so much the more, as ye see the day approaching.

If more church *boards* allowed the Holy Spirit to move,
our churches would have fewer *bored* meetings.

Acts 6:3
Wherefore, brethren, look ye out among you seven
men of honest report, full of the Holy Ghost and
wisdom, whom we may appoint over this business.

God didn't call you to be *typical*.
He called you to be *Biblical*.

1 Peter 2:9
But you are a chosen generation, a royal priesthood,
a holy nation, His own special people, that you may
proclaim the praises of Him who called you out of
darkness into His marvelous light.

For Christians to *glow* in the dark, we have to *grow* in
the light.

2 Peter 1:19
And so we have the prophetic word confirmed, which you do well to heed as a light that shines in a dark place, until the day dawns and the morning star rises in your hearts;

1 John 1:7
But if we walk in the light, as he is in the light, we have fellowship with one another, and the blood of Jesus, his Son, purifies us from all sin.

As a Christian, your life is either an *oracle* of God or an *article* about God.

I preached this thought at Word of Life yesterday. Very few people are an oracle of God, meaning they are a spokesperson to tell others what God is saying.

However, every Christian is an article about God. Unbelievers, as well as other Christians, read our lives. Does what they read from our lives truly represent Jesus? I feel it's imperative for every article that we post on social media (or whatever people see us do) should represent true Christianity.

Whether you are an oracle or an article, people need to see Christ in your conversation.

1 Peter 4:11
If any man speak, let him speak as the oracles of God; if any man minister, let him do it as of the ability which God giveth: that God in all things may be glorified through Jesus Christ, to whom be praise

and dominion for ever and ever.

2 Corinthians 3:2-3
Ye are our epistle written in our hearts, known and read of all men: Forasmuch as ye are manifestly declared to be the epistle of Christ ministered by us, written not with ink, but with the Spirit of the living God; not in tables of stone, but in fleshy tables of the heart.

It's okay to be right and know it, but it's not okay to be rude and show it.

Being rude about someone who is wrong is just as wrong as them not being right.

Ephesians 4:32
Be kind to one another, tenderhearted, forgiving one another, as God in Christ forgave you.

As long as I can remember, Teachers emphasized the difference between can I and may I.

It is proper to ask, "May I?"

"May I?" is asking permission to do something. With that in mind, this morning, I thought about this verse:

Psalm 30:5
For his anger endures but a moment; in his favor is life: weeping *may* endure for a night, but joy comes

in the morning.

No matter what your situation is today, weeping only has permission to last through the night because joy has been commissioned to come in the morning.

The Church was designed for the world to see the beauty of Christ-in the body of Christ, Who is the Church.

Christianity is not the *absence of problems*; it's the *presence of purpose*.

God desires to be your *first response*, not your *last resort*. (But, He will still hear you as a last resort.)

People that are inclusive of different races often say that they are colorblind. Out of all due respect, that is not a great statement.

Embracing people with a different color of skin is the real sign of a lack of prejudice.

Being able to see a difference without making a difference is a quality of true Christianity.

Ephesians 2:13-14
But now in Christ Jesus ye who sometimes were far off are made nigh by the blood of Christ.
For he is our peace, who hath made both one, and hath broken down the middle wall of partition between us;

There will always be a race problem as long as we leave the "g" off.

If we will put the "g" back in front and again show grace, there will never be a race problem.

Titus 2:11
For the grace of God that brings salvation has appeared to all men.

A race is people you *run with*, not people you *run from* because of differences.

A true Christian should never *discriminate* against people nor publicly *incriminate* a person.

As a Christian, it is your God-given mandate to help erase the race issue. If we continue on the existing pages of life to write what is not right, History will continue to repeat itself.

If every "race" of people would deal with the cause of the sin, we could get past the color of the skin.

When you let certain people *set* the table but won't let them sit at the table, you have a wrong mindset.

As a Christian, one of the fundamental beliefs that I have is the power of baptism. The Bible declares that baptism is for the remission of sin. That is ALL sin, not just the sins that we pick and choose. One of the sins of our society is RACISM. I believe that the SIN of RACISM is drowned in the waters of BAPTISM.

When you rise to walk in newness of life after you are baptized, you realize that by ONE spirit are we all baptized into ONE body.

> 1 Corinthians 12:13
> For by one Spirit are we all baptized into one body, whether we be Jews or Gentiles, whether we be bond or free; and have been all made to drink into one Spirit.

Chapter 3
Closer to Home

Parents have many challenging roles. One of them is teaching each child how to have a *backbone* without being a *bully*.

> Proverbs 22:6
> Train up a child in the way he should go: and when he is old, he will not depart from it.

> Romans 12:18
> If it is possible, as much as depends on you, live peaceably with all men.

At the end of your life, your family needs to see your imprints where you *walked with them* and not your footprints where you *walked on them*.

It doesn't matter if your *fans* follow you and call you a *legend* if your *family* doesn't follow you and want your *legacy*.

Sir, your wife and kids don't need you to be *Super Man*; they need you to be home for *supper, man*.

Mam, your husband and kids don't need you to be *Wonder Woman*. They should never have to *wonder* where you are.

A *smartphone* should never replace a *smart parent*.

Your kids need *unlimited Daddy* more than they need *unlimited data*.

Nowadays, kids learn to use *data* before they learn to say, "*Daddy.*"

Having a child is a significant *milestone*.
Harming a child deserves a great *millstone*.
Matthew 18:1-6

At the same time came the disciples unto Jesus, saying, Who is the greatest in the kingdom of heaven? And Jesus called a little child unto him, and set him in the midst of them, and said, Verily I say unto you, Except ye be converted, and become as little children, ye shall not enter into the kingdom of heaven. Whosoever therefore shall humble himself as this little child, the same is greatest in the kingdom of heaven. And whoso shall receive one such little child in my name receives me. But whoso shall offend one of these little ones which believe in me, it were better for him that a millstone were hanged about his neck, and that he were drowned in the depth of the sea.

Your worth is not written in a *ledger*.
It is etched in a *legacy*.

2 Timothy 1:5
When I call to remembrance the unfeigned faith that is in thee, which dwelt first in thy grandmother Lois, and thy mother Eunice; and I am persuaded that in thee also.

Usually, when a story begins with the four words, "*Once upon a time*," it is a *fable*.

Always, when a story begins with the four words, "*In the beginning, God*," it is a *fact*.

One hundred years from now, someone will casually mention your name. They will tell their children about you, their ancestor.

If I could choose the four words that would begin that conversation about me, I pray that it will be, "In the beginning, God," not "Once upon a time."

I want my life to be a fact not a fable.

It's amazing that I hear parents say, "My kids will not listen to me!" Then, I hear the kids say exactly what they listened to the parents say, words the parents wished the kids had not heard.

People are amusing creatures. In pre-marriage counseling, I've heard countless people say, "I'm *crazy about* my fiancé." Then, those same people came back later for after-marriage counseling and said, "I'm *crazy because* of my spouse."

I guess there are different kinds of crazy.

You learn how to parent just as soon as your kids are grown. That makes you smart enough to tell your kids how they should raise your grandkids.

Don't roll your eyes when an adult says, "When I was a kid." In the blink of an eye, you will be saying it too.

Not long after the potty training is finished, the training wheels are started.

One of my great joys when the kids were little was teaching them how to ride a bike. Once they grew very comfortable with the training wheels on, I removed them.

Embedded in my mind, I have an image of running behind each of them to catch them when they lost their balance. Yes, there were a few wobbles and an occasional tumble, but the ultimate goal was met. It wasn't long until they were riding faster than I could run behind them. And guess what? They can all still ride a bike.

That encourages me. The Bible is also encouraging when it says in Proverbs 22:6 to "train up a child in the way he should go: and when he is old, he will not depart from it."

If my children and yours still remember how we trained them to balance a bike, don't think for one minute that they don't know how we trained them to live by the balance of the Bible. No matter how many wobbles and tumbles they've had, the training is still embedded in their minds.

So, if you are a young parent and your kids are still small, keep training! The balance on the bicycle will help them to learn to balance life.

And if your kids are grown, keep believing! If they still remember how to ride a bike, they still remember all of the other training you did too. Soon their train will get back on track, and they will remember the balance you taught them from the Bible!

A real legacy is when your kids remember more about what you *taught 'em* than what you *bought 'em*.

I'm not a relationship guru, and I'm not against a public display of affection for your honey. But, relationships are not about how you *tweet* your spouse in public, but how you *treat* them in private.

They need to see your *face*, not just your *Facebook* post.

As I sat at the park last night, I saw a grandfather "racing" his three-year-old granddaughter. And of course, this little child left her grandfather in the dust. Obviously, it was a setup. As an observer, remembering the many, many times that I had done that with my children, my mind began to race much faster than they were running.

As adults, from the time that kids can barely run, we let them win every race. With a lifetime achievement award smile on his face, that little toddler feels like the best runner and the fastest in the world.

Then, life happens in the real world, and the kids that we have let win, lose for the first time.

In despair, they call Santa Claus, and obviously he doesn't answer. They call the Easter Bunny, and apparently he has hopped away. Maybe the tooth fairy has a little "pull." No. Cinderella? Prince Charming? Elsa?

No, no, and no!

Then, someone says, "What about Jesus?"

As a last resort, they open the Bible as if it's an emergency. They turn to Ecclesiastes 9:11 and read, "The race is not to the swift, nor the battle to the strong."

As they read further, they find out that Jesus has already won every race. With a sigh of relief, for the first time in their lives, they realize no one has to let them win. With Jesus taking first place in their life, they know that number One has already won.

You should always be *transparent* because the people that call you *Parent* know who you really are.

A Dad does not babysit! He raises the child that he fathered.

The space between *"too young"* and *"too old"* is way *"too short."*

It doesn't matter if you come from a long line of *lovers* or a long line of *losers*. Accepting Christ puts you in the genealogy of Jesus. After you accept the blood of Jesus, you have the DNA of Deity.

You are not an *accident* looking for a place to happen. You are a *purpose* designed to show others what is happening.

I've heard verbally abusive parents tell their children that when they were born they were an *accident*.

I've also heard people, in a joking manner, tell someone else that they are an *accident waiting to happen.*

If either of these "accident" incidents has ever been spoken over you, you don't have to believe either one! You weren't an accident when you were born! You are fearfully and wonderfully made, and you are not an accident now looking for a place to happen.

In both cases, you are a purpose happening now.

Happily ever after only happens when you live every day like never before.

My Family Tree is shaped like a cross.

My genealogy is connected to my Theology.

Even though I am a Gentile, I traced my roots back to Israel. When I "climbed" my family tree, I found that my genealogy is connected to my Theology. Jesus Himself said that He is the Root and offspring of David, and I am His child.

However, my Family tree is the shape of a cross. My roots are under a tree on a hill at Golgotha. It's better known as Calvary. Jesus was my Father's Father's Father's Father's Father's Father's Father, back for many generations. But through the power of the bloodline, He became my Father too. No, you won't find this information on an ancestry website, but you will discover it in the Bible. Why don't you look up your Family tree? If you have accepted the One who died on the tree, you will find out that we are kin because of the cross!

Weddings begin with a *Wow* and end with a *Vow*.

Marriages begin with a *Vow*, and it's up to you to keep the *Wow* in it.

When you train your kids in truth, it is similar to teaching them to ride a bicycle. Most kids learn to ride a bike, and then they lose interest when they start driving a car. But on any given day, if they were forced to ride a bike, they could get on and take off.

The same is true with the truth. Your children may lose interest about the time they start driving a car. But on any given day, if they are forced to remember the truth, it will come back to them.

It's a promise from God.

Proverbs 22:6
Train up a child in the way he should go: and when he is old, he will not depart from it.

This is from a Dad that witnessed the training wheels come off of bikes and a Dad that trained my kids in truth. They may not still ride bikes, and they may not do everything right, but on any given day, they remember how.

Truth is like a time-release capsule. You give it to your children when they are young. After a certain age, it will release.

Children need to be *commanded*, but they also need to be *commended*.

Now and then, an *attaboy* or *attagirl* thrown at them will brighten their world. And, it's been proven that if you will accentuate the positive, it will help offset the negative.

(Oh and by the way, this works for adults too.)

You can't be *chained* to what your *ancestors* did while you try to *change* what your *descendants* will do.

Even if your marriage was a *match* made in heaven, you still need to *strike* up a conversation with your spouse.

It's okay to call your chocolate hot, but *beautiful* is a much classier term to call your wife.

If you are a *parrot*, you repeat things. If you are a *parent*, you repeat things.

She stole my heart, but I forgave her and let her keep it.

The only way that rain will ruin your relationship is if you do not use the same umbrella.

Okay, guys.

If you want to be a real man, you need to stop being a *player* and start being a *prayer*.

> James 5:16
> The effectual fervent prayer of a righteous man avails much.

The problem with blaming all of your problems on your ancestors is that your descendants will follow in your footsteps. Soon you will be the ancestor that they blame their problems on.

Marriage is an investment that is funded by daily *interest*.

Children look up to adults for their *depth*, not their *height*.

> John 13:15

For I have given you an example, that ye should do as I have done to you.

A child's self-worth is more determined by what's said by a *parent* than what's said at a *pageant*.

It's both a positive and a negative connotation when someone says, "It runs in the family."

From dying of old age to getting sick at a young age, people say it runs in the family. From good looks to bad luck and money to morals, this statement "runs in families."

But, as a leader for many years, I've heard this statement used negatively more than positively, especially with "D" words: Disease, dysfunction, depression, disorder, drugs, diet, and on and on. In my opinion, someone needs to break the cycle and not be afraid to "walk away from" what "runs in the family."

How do you do that? You get tired of the darkness and ask the Lord to help you to walk in the Light.

1 John 1:7
But if we walk in the light, as he is in the light, we have fellowship one with another, and the blood of Jesus Christ his Son cleanseth us from all sin.

1 Peter 2:9
But you are a chosen people, a royal priesthood, a holy nation.

You should never hear a preacher say, "Do not try this at home."

The church is where your faith is *refined*, and home is where your faith is *defined*.

If you want your kids to be on the *Honor Roll*, display a *role of honor* in your home.

Legacies live on long after dynasties die out.

We have a generation that watched so much of *Saved by the Bell*, but they don't know they were *saved* by the *blood*.

Exposing your kids to dysfunction and praying that it doesn't affect them is like sticking your hand in the fire and hoping you will not get burned.

Child support will buy your child's *food*.

Moral support would build your child's *future*.

You can live in the same home as your kids and still be an absentee parent. While it's important to work and provide for your family, it's also important to prioritize your kids over all of your favorite hobbies.

In the story of the birth of Jesus, Joseph was just as important as Mary. Few men nowadays show his integrity. He put all of his natural feelings aside for about a year to stand with Mary through her pregnancy with a baby that was not his, biologically. His loyalty made him a mirror image of how earthly fathers are supposed to reflect the image of the Heavenly Father.

When Joseph found out that Mary was having a baby that was *not his*, he decided to *stay*.

These days, a lot of guys find out that their gal is having a baby that *is his* and they *leave*.

Crawl. Walk. Fall. Crawl. Walk. Fall. Crawl. Walk. Fall. Crawl. Walk. Run. Walk. Run. Walk. Run. Fall. Crawl. Walk. Crawl. Walk. Run. Fall. Walk.

I think you get the gist. When we begin our lives as infants, and our parents finally put us down, out of nowhere, we start crawling, along with much applause. Before you know it, we pull up on the coffee table and waddle, then walk, receiving much higher praise. But then, we fall again, so we crawl again. Then, we forget about the fall and walk again, and before you know it, our parents are shouting, "Stop running in this house!"

As I walked this morning, I decided to share a little of my story. I usually stay very private about personal matters, because as a pastor, I see stories that are so much worse than mine. However, I feel that there is a lesson in my story that many can relate to in life.

In 1989, I had my first back surgery. As embarrassing as it was, as a 29-year old with a ruptured disc, I experienced crawling again after 28 years of walking and running. However, after that first surgery, I recovered very well. But after ten years, that unwelcome pain ran down my spine and my leg. After trying physical therapy and just all out being brave, I was more than ready for relief. So in 1999, I joyfully agreed to yet another back surgery. Post-surgery, I remember waking up pain-free. After a few days of recovery, I was well on my way. In fact, I preached the first sermon in our new Church building five days after surgery!

For the first time in a long time, at 39, I felt so good. It was during this time that I developed a passion for running. My life went like this: Eat. Run. Eat. Run. Eat. Run.

Running was as good for me mentally as it was physically. It became a big part of my prayer life, as I would run with no phone and no one to talk to but God.

There were times that I would run with my son, and I watched him develop a passion for running also. (Now he runs marathons.)

For 17 years, I ran and was relatively pain-free. But then, there was the dog. The dog in my neighborhood on a road that I usually never ran. As he barked, growled, and showed me his teeth, and was on my heels, I panicked, tripped, and fell. I quickly went from running to bleeding to limping to yes...crawling.

Of course, I was more frustrated than I was injured, or so I thought. But then, the pain would not go away. I began injections, therapy, and on and on. I would get better for a while then get worse.

As a private person that lives a public life, back problems are something you can't hide. I would go to the mall with Ann and have to sit down every few minutes.

So after a year of this misery, I tracked down my neurosurgeon. He immediately saw the problem on my MRI and said he was sure he could help me. He gave me three choices: 1) Continue to hurt. 2) Keep getting injections. 3) Surgery.

I chose number 3.

So, in June of last year, I had my third back surgery. As I awoke from the surgery, I wasn't pain-free, but I felt so much better. I had to remind myself that I was 56 and not quite as young as I used to be. However, after a few weeks, I began to live pain-free again. After about a month, I asked my doctor if I could run again. He said to start by walking, so I did. And it felt SO good. When I went back again, my doctor said, "You can start running now, but be smart."

Well, to me, *be smart* meant that as long as I was not hurting, I should keep running. Within a month I was back up to 4-5 miles a day, averaging 25 miles a week. And because I could run, I did other things too, including lifting and bending. Then, it happened again.

The day after Labor Day, I could hardly walk, and I sure couldn't run. After weeks of pain, I agreed to yet another MRI. Excruciating leg pain and walking all bent over made me very frustrated, so, back to the back doctor I went. He said, "Let's give it a little more time."

I'm so thankful for his wisdom because it gave God a bit more time to bring healing also.

Today, I am much better. The leg pain is 90% gone, and my back is only sore.

Remember at the beginning of this writing I said-this morning as I was walking?

Here's the main reason I felt to write this blog. My Dad is a 76-year-old wise man. He is a man of few words, so when he speaks, I feel a great need to heed. Not long ago, he said to me, "I think you need to stop running. I feel like you are creating damage by the beating on the pavement."

I admit those words stung a little because I love to run. But, I love my Dad more, and the Bible teaches me that I need to honor him. Yes, I know I'm grown and I'm a 57-year- old man, but I am heeding his advice. I want to live to be an old man, and God has promised me if I honor my father and my mother that my days will be long. So, until my dad tells me I can run again, I will walk. Yes, I will walk as fast as I can without breaking into a jog.

When I was running regularly, I indeed wasn't the fastest. But I did run a 26-minute 5k, which is about an 8-minute, 40-second mile. Today, I walked a 5k distance with a 14-minute, 56-second mile. Yes, it took me almost twice as long, but I feel good, and I know that I am on my way to being pain-free. I'm not just enhancing my physical health, but I am using this time also to pray and strengthen my walk with the Lord. I may never get "permission" to run again, but thank God I can walk!

Now, the spiritual application that I want to give you is this: As you crawl, walk, fall, crawl, walk, run, fall, and walk throughout your life, listen to your Heavenly Father as well as your earthly father. Remember that He knows all about every-thing that you are facing. Also, remember that there are thousands of people that would love to trade problems with you because all of us are living out our own life lessons.

It's my prayer for all of you, no matter what cross you are bearing, that you know your Heavenly Father doesn't require you to be the fastest; but, He does require you to finish. And even though I can't fulfill all of this verse right now, it is still God's Word.

Isaiah 40:31 says, "But they that wait upon the Lord shall renew their strength; they shall mount up with wings as eagles; they shall run, and not be weary, and they shall walk and not faint."

All I can do now is walk. But I will walk and not faint as I wait on my Heavenly Father to renew my strength; so I can eventually mount up with wings as eagles, run, and not be weary.

And when my Heavenly Father gives me that strength, I know my earthly father will be listening, and he will say, "RUN, TOMMY, RUN."

Chapter 4
Hope for the Holidays

J esus had just been cruelly crucified at Calvary. Three days later, the media reported that He was missing from the grave. Some of His disciples were walking and talking about these events when a "Stranger" stepped up. As they walked on the road to Emmaus, He walked them through the Old Testament, from Moses to the Prophets, giving them all of the verses about Him.

When they arrived at their destination, He made as though He would go farther, but they invited Him in.

As the custom was, they asked their "Guest" to pray. So, as He had done many other times, He took the bread, blessed it, and brake it, and gave it to them. When He did that, the Scripture says they knew Him.

My prayer for all of my friends is that you would get the chance to walk with Jesus this year. Let Him expound His Word to you and reveal Himself to you personally. The most excellent New Year that you can ever have is a year in which you can say, "Jesus appeared to me, and we walked and talked together-and I knew Him!"

Happy *Knew* Year!

Luke 24:31
And their eyes were opened, and they knew Him, and
He vanished out of their sight.

Unto *us* a child is born, unto *us*, a Son is given...

The preceding verse is one of my all-time favorite verses,
even when it's not Christmas.

However, when some people hear the word *us*, they stop
listening. For thousands of people, there is no *us*. It's just them,
all *alone*.

Even though I have never seen the program, one of the most
popular television shows now is **This Is Us**. Sadly, in the midst
of their holiday loneliness, many people look at us and dream
of what it would be like to be like us.

If you are one of those lonely people this Christmas Day,
or any day of the year, I have great news for you! When the
angels announced the birth of the Child that was born and the
Son that was given, they did not say *us*.

The angels said, "Unto *you* is born this day in the city of
David a Savior, which is Christ the Lord."

Today, you need to personalize the fact of all that God has
done for you. Just after the Church was birthed in Acts, Peter
said "for the promise is unto *you*"…that's all of *us*.

When you realize that Jesus did what He did for you,
it's easier to handle hearing, "Merry Christmas to *you* from
all of *us*."

The most excellent way to share the *birth* in Bethlehem is with the *rebirth* that happened in you.

Luke 2:11
For unto you is born this day in the city of David a Savior, which is Christ the Lord.

1 Peter 1:23
Being born again, not of corruptible seed, but of incorruptible, by the word of God, which lives and abides forever.

Unto us, a *Son* is *given*;
Unto us, our *sin* is *forgiven*.

Isaiah 9:6
For unto us a child is born, unto us a son is given: and the government shall be upon his shoulder: and his name shall be called Wonderful, Counsellor, The mighty God, The everlasting Father, The Prince of Peace.

Luke 5:20
And when he saw their faith, he said unto him, Man, thy sins are forgiven thee.

Luke 7:48
And he said unto her, Thy sins are forgiven.

Christmas is about Jesus coming the *first time* to get people ready for when He comes back the *second time*.

Hebrews 9:28
So Christ was once offered to bear the sins of many; and unto them that look for him shall he appear the second time without sin unto salvation.

Christmas is about Jesus coming to an *unstable* world to give us a *stable* environment.

James 1:8
A double minded man is unstable in all his ways.

1 Chronicles 16:30
Fear before him, all the earth: the world also shall be stable, that it be not moved.

The first time Jesus came, He came to a *stable*. The next time He comes will be on a *stallion*.

Luke 2: 7
And she brought forth her firstborn son, and wrapped him in swaddling clothes, and laid him in a manger; because there was no room for them in the inn.

Revelation 6:2
And I saw, and behold a white horse: and he that sat on him had a bow; and a crown was given unto him: and he went forth conquering, and to conquer.

Wise men don't *wish* upon a star. They *follow* it.

Matthew 2:2, 9
Saying, Where is he that is born King of the Jews? for we have seen his star in the east, and are come to worship him.

When they had heard the king, they departed; and, lo, the star, which they saw in the east, went before them, till it came and stood over where the young child was.

You don't need to thank your lucky stars. You need to follow the star to Bethlehem.

Matthew 2:9-10
When they had heard the king, they departed; and, lo, the star, which they saw in the east, went before them,

till it came and stood over where the young child was. When they saw the star, they rejoiced with exceeding great joy.

On the first day of Christmas, my true love sent to me, His only Begotten Son.

I don't need the gifts from the other 11 days.

God didn't send an *email*. He sent *a Male*. His name is Jesus. Have you received Him?

Good Will is more than a *store*; it's the *story* of redemption.

Luke 2:14
Glory to God in the highest, and on earth peace, good will toward men.

You usually won't find the Christmas *story* at the Christmas *store*.

Before you give your kids the stuff from the retail store, retell them the real story of Christmas.

The greatest gift of all time will not be found *under* a tree. He was found *on* one.

One of the fun things about Christmas is gift wrap. Experienced wrappers carefully create pretty packages. But no matter how pretty the package, the inside of the box is what has our interest. The gift is under the wrap.

But have you ever looked under the wrap and found there was nothing in the box?

Obviously, there is no greater gift than the True Gift of Christmas, which is Christ. When He was born, His mother wrapped Him in swaddling clothes. Then when He died, Joseph took Him down from the cross and wrapped His body in linen. Underneath the swaddling clothes and the linen, the greatest gift of all time was wrapped.

But then I find it very interesting that Jesus knew how to wrap and unwrap. On the third day, when the disciples came to the tomb, they found the wrap but couldn't find the gift.

John 20:6-7
Then comes Simon Peter following him, and went into the sepulchre, and sees the linen clothes lie, and the napkin, that was about his head, not lying with the linen clothes, but wrapped together in a place by itself.

The God of glory who wrapped Himself in flesh was now unwrapped. He ascended back to heaven and sent back to us the gift of the Holy Spirit.

It is my prayer during this Christmas season that we will not keep the gift under wrap but display Him for all the world to see.

Easter was never meant to be about an egg that you chose to *dye*; it's about a Lamb that chose to *die*.

1.2 million American soldiers have laid down and died so we could pick up and move on.

After any trauma, fragmented families have to find a way to pick up and move on. Since our great country began, 1.2 million military families have had to "pick up and move on" without their family member.

That person is not just a statistic; they were someone's son or daughter or Dad or Mother. Thanks to the freedoms they fought for, you and I are still "moving on" in America. And one of the freedoms they died to give us was free speech.

So, every time you speak, remember someone died for you to be able to say that. It's okay to disagree with a political party, but it's not okay to disrespect the soldiers that departed.

I don't know if *three times* will *charm* you, but I do know *three days* will *change* you!

Mark 8:31
And he began to teach them, that the Son of man must suffer many things, and be rejected of the elders, and

of the chief priests, and scribes, and be killed, and
after three days rise again.

There's no need to take *flowers* to the grave of Jesus.
He's already *a ROSE*.
Solomon 2:1
I am the Rose of Sharon...

In Arlington National Cemetery, armed guards are still
guarding The Tomb of the *Unknown* Soldier.
In Jerusalem, the armed guards left the tomb, because the
One in the tomb left too.
I'm glad I know who was in the tomb of the *known* soldier.

Friday is sad,
Saturday is gloom,
But hang around to Sunday, and you'll find an empty tomb!

JESUS IS DEAD...
At least that's what they said.
The hopes of all the disciples had been diminished,
As Jesus hung His head and said, *It is finished*.
In all of hell, there wasn't a frown,

As Joseph and Nicodemus took Jesus down.
They took Him and placed Him in a borrowed tomb,
And said their goodbyes, forever they assumed.
But listen, all of you people, and remember what He said,
In just three days I won't be dead.
I know Friday is sad, and Saturday is gloom,
But hang around until Sunday, and you will find an empty tomb.
I'll come out alive after dying for your sin,
I've looked at the devil and said, *I win*.
I've taken the keys of the grave, death, and hell,
And the first thing I want from you is for you to go tell.
Tell it in the country and tell it in all nations,
Jesus is alive after dying for your salvation.
If you will go to Jerusalem and make a brand new start,
I'll fill you with My Spirit and give you a brand new heart.
I will fill the whole earth with my glory,
As you tell everybody the redemption story.
In a world full of turmoil, where sin does abound,
I will pour out my grace, and the lost will be found.
I will give you joy and lots of laughter,
And show you the true meaning of *happily ever after*.
Just like I came out of the grave, so will all the saints.
I'll take you to Heaven, and forever you will dance.
You'll praise and sing on streets of pure gold.
You'll live forever and never grow old.
And just to think, you would truly be lost,
Had I not gone to the old rugged cross.
If I had not said, *It is finished*,
All of your hopes would truly have been diminished.
But because of the price I paid for your sin,
We're together forever, and there's never an end!

Good Friday is a time of *mourning*.
But all of that changes on Sunday *morning*!

There's an age-old question that asks, "Why do bad things happen to good people?"

Easter should be the best answer to that question. Something horrible happened to the best Guy ever. Every sin that everybody had ever committed was piled on His back. He was beaten, bruised, spit on, mocked, ridiculed, nailed, and had a crown of thorns smashed deep into His brow-just to name a few of the bad things.

It was terrible. But, we call it Good Friday.

Bad things do happen to good people. But if that were not the case, you and I would never have a good day. Now we have a good life, thanks to Good Friday!

You can't keep a *God-man* down.

It's okay to put all your eggs in one basket because all of your hope was placed in one tomb.

Sometimes the best of times and the worst of times are only three days apart.

Ask Jesus!

Color the eggs, but don't camouflage the agony.

I'm *grateful* for a *faithful* God!

> Lamentations 3:22-23
> It is of the Lord's mercies that we are not consumed, because his compassions fail not. They are new every morning: Great is thy faithfulness.

Too far down to give thanks:

So, you think that you are so far down that Thanksgiving seems impossible?

Well, before you drown yourself in the dismal doom of your depravity, let me tell you about a brother in the Lord who maybe had it a touch worse than you.

He was an incredible evangelist in whom God put a lot of stock. He told God that he would do anything, so God put him to the test. God asked him to go and preach in a very hostile environment where wickedness was rampant. This test scared my brother so badly that unfortunately, he refused to go. From that day forward, he faced the downward spiral of deterioration.

The calm that he was used to feeling turned into a storm that rocked his world, as well as the boat that he was escaping on. In fact, things got so bad that he asked people to help him die. He had gone so far overboard in his *faith* that now he felt going overboard was his *fate*.

Sadly, his disobedience didn't only affect him. It affected everyone around him. He literally had placed the lives of innocent people on the line, and death was imminent-not just for him, but for all with whom he rubbed shoulders.

Literally, as a last resort, the people on the ship threw him overboard. Death was seemingly certain, but what's sadder than death was the way he was drowning, not just in water, but in the waste of the giftings and talents with which he had been endowed.

But then as his life flashed before his eyes, so did a huge fish. Amazingly, a fragmented man who was far from being whole was swallowed whole.

(I think you know by now that my brother in the Lord is an acquaintance of yours too. His familiar name is Jonah.)

Jonah was now in the belly of a whale, but to hear him tell it, it was the belly of hell (Jonah 2:2). He was as far down as a man could go. He had fulfilled what the Psalmist said in Psalm 139:7-8. "Where shall I go from your spirit and where shall I flee from your presence?

If I make my bed in hell, you are there."

And was God ever there!

With weeds wrapped around his head, he began to wrap God around his heart again. In the middle of misery, he was in the middle of mercy! What a powerful prayer he prayed in the most unlikely place.

But then, he stopped praying and started praising God. His exact words were, "I will sacrifice unto you with the voice of THANKSGIVING."

Immediately after this pledge of praise, the whale vomited Jonah up on the dry ground. And Jonah hit the ground running. This awful, awesome experience helped him to coin the phrase, "making up for lost time."

He made a three-day journey in one day and preached to the people from whom he had tried to escape.

I have been down before, but probably not quite that far down. But, I have learned the verse that says, "In everything give thanks, for this is the will of God in Christ Jesus concerning you."

I don't know how far down you are today, but I do know that you are not so far down that God will not hear you. I want to provoke you for just a moment to think about how good God has been to you. I assure you-when you start to think, you will start to thank.

Like Jonah, you too, in the middle of your misery, will find yourself in the middle of God's mercy, and you will be able to say, "Happy Thanksgiving!"

Show me a man who *thinks*, and I'll show you a man who *thanks*.

1 Thessalonians 5:18
In every thing give thanks: for this is the will of God
in Christ Jesus concerning you.

In the South, we call in *DRESSING*. In the Midwest, they
call it *STUFFING*.

But no matter what you call it, the next day when you start
DRESSING, you find yourself *STUFFING* an extra couple of
pounds into your clothes.

Happy Thanksgiving!

THANKSGIVING:

A day to be thankful for what you've *got*, not what you are
going to *get* a month from now on Christmas.

A "WHOLE" lot of THANKS:

In the 17th chapter of Luke, there is a fantastic Thanksgiving
story. Ten men were lepers that asked Jesus to have mercy on
them. Jesus immediately instructed them to go show themselves to the Priest in obedience to the Law.

However, as they merely obeyed Jesus, each of them looked
down and discovered that they had been healed. Nine of them
ran to their family and shared the good news. But the other one
ran back and tracked Jesus down. When he saw Him, the man
bowed down and began to give Him THANKS.

Jesus asked him where all of his buddies were. He simply said, "I can't speak for them, but I just had to come by and give thanks."

What Jesus said then amazes me. He looked at him and said, "Your faith has made you WHOLE."

The ex-leper was healed by obedience, but he was made whole by praise.

Giving of thanks gave him the power not only to be healed but for him to be restored from everything the disease had taken away!

A WHOLE lot of people need to give Jesus a WHOLE lot of praise. I am believing for a lot of healing during the holidays, for as we give thanks, Jesus makes WHOLE.

Saying thanks is something you do for a moment.
Giving thanks is what you should do for a lifetime.

All of us have prayed for the will of God in our lives. At times it seems like it's a mysterious plan a million miles away. If you are like me, you have often thought how incredible it would be to have someone to tell you without a doubt what that will of God is.

If you have ever felt that way, today is your day! I know what God's will is for your life.

His will for your life is found in 1Thessalonians 5:18: "In every thing give thanks: for THIS IS THE WILL OF GOD in Christ Jesus CONCERNING YOU."

It doesn't get any more plain than that. During the month of Thanksgiving and every other month as well, take the time to give God thanks IN everything.

I have heard people misquote this verse from 1 Thessalonians. They say the Bible says, "FOR everything give thanks." Accordingly, I've heard people thank God for their sickness, thank God for their dysfunction and disappointment, and on and on.

But, the correct word is IN. Thank God IN your illness. IN your despair. IN your times of mourning. And as we praise Him IN these times, we discover His will for our lives.

Some people are so *cheap* they won't even *give* thanks.

Chapter 5
Encouragement

Your *highest hopes* are usually not experienced until after your *deepest hurts*.

> Philippians 1:19
> For I know that this shall turn to my salvation through your prayer, and the supply of the Spirit of Jesus Christ.

No matter what you are *undergoing*, you are not *going under*-if you will trust in God.

Undergoing is the process of *overcoming*!

> Isaiah 43:2
> When you pass through the waters, I will be with you; And through the rivers, they shall not overflow you. When you walk through the fire, you shall not

be burned, Nor shall the flame scorch you.

Psalm 23:4
Yea, though I walk through the valley of the shadow
of death, I will fear no evil: for thou art with me; thy
rod and thy staff they comfort me.

When Jesus was in the wilderness being tempted by the
devil, the keyword that was used by the enemy was *if.*

If you are the Son of God.

But all three times the devil used the two-letter word *if,*
Jesus came back with a two-letter word of His own. Every time
satan said *if,* Jesus said *it.*

It is written.

The devil is still busy with throwing up the word *if* to all
of God's children. *If* you were really a Christian; *If* God really
loved you; and on and on the *if's* continue.

But I encourage you to answer the enemy like Jesus: *It*
is written.

Find promises in God's Word that He has made to you, and
tell the devil like *it* is!

Luke 4:1-13
And Jesus being full of the Holy Ghost returned from
Jordan, and was led by the Spirit into the wilderness,
being forty days tempted of the devil. And in those
days he did eat nothing: and when they were ended,
he afterward hungered. And the devil said unto him,
If thou be the Son of God, command this stone that

it be made bread. And Jesus answered him, saying, It is written, That man shall not live by bread alone, but by every word of God. And the devil, taking him up into an high mountain, showed unto him all the kingdoms of the world in a moment of time. And the devil said unto him, All this power will I give thee, and the glory of them: for that is delivered unto me; and to whomsoever I will I give it. If thou therefore wilt worship me, [1] all shall be thine. And Jesus answered and said unto him, Get thee behind me, Satan: for it is written, Thou shalt worship the Lord thy God, and him only shalt thou serve. And he brought him to Jerusalem, and set him on a pinnacle of the temple, and said unto him, If thou be the Son of God, cast thyself down from hence: For it is written, He shall give his angels charge over thee, to keep thee: And in their hands they shall bear thee up, lest at any time thou dash thy foot against a stone. And Jesus answering said unto him, It is said, Thou shalt not tempt the Lord thy God. And when the devil had ended all the temptation, he departed from him for a season.

There are a lot of scriptures about "long" nights.

Job 7:3-4
Wearisome are appointed to me. When I lie down, I say, When shall I arise, and the night be gone? and I am full of tossings to and fro unto the dawning

of the day.

Psalm 6:6
I am weary with my groaning; all the night make I my
bed to swim; I water my couch with my tears.

But there are also scriptures about the majesty of the morning.

Psalm 30:5
...weeping may endure for a night, but joy comes in
the morning.

And then there's my favorite.

Lamentations 3:21-23
This I recall to my mind, therefore have I hope. It
is of the Lord's mercies that we are not consumed,
because his compassions fail not. They are new every
morning: great is thy faithfulness.

God has a guarantee.
For every *night of misery*, there is a new *morning of mercy*.

When the world writes you *off*, the Lord writes you *in*...the
Lamb's Book of Life.

Luke 10:20
Notwithstanding in this rejoice not, that the spirits
are subject unto you; but rather rejoice, because your

names are written in heaven.

Revelation 21:27
But there shall by no means enter it anything that
defiles, or causes an abomination or a lie, but only
those who are written in the Lamb's Book of Life.

The devil has a strategy to destroy you. But no worries,
Jesus is *stronger* than his *strategy*.

John 10:10
The thief comes not, but for to steal, and to kill, and
to destroy: I am come that they might have life, and
that they might have it more abundantly.

The toughest part of Pastoring is coaching people through
their toughest times. Unexpected death and sickness catch a lot
of people by surprise. From infants to those in their nineties,
the challenge is always great.

As a young Pastor, I felt like I was supposed to be able to
calm all fears and dry all tears. But one of the things that I have
learned after 40 years in the ministry is this: Rarely do people
find every piece *of* a broken heart. But always, if they put their
trust in Christ, they have peace *in* their broken hearts.

Isaiah 26:3
You will keep him in perfect peace, Whose mind is stayed on You Because he trusts in You.

Don't let a *short stall* affect the *long haul*.

Ecclesiastes 9:11
I returned, and saw under the sun, that the race is not to the swift, nor the battle to the strong.

We all go through things in life, but the key is going *through* while you are going *to*.

Your *situation* is not your *destination*!

Jesus got in the boat with disciples and said, "Let's go to the other side." The other side was their destination. But while they were en route, they faced a situation. A horrible storm came, and they thought they were going to die. When they called on Jesus, their situation changed, and they safely landed at their destination.

Today, no matter what you are going through, remember where you are going to. Even the valley of the shadow of death is not a destination; it's a situation.

The Psalmist told us in Psalm 23, "Yea, though I walk through the valley of the shadow of death, You are with me..."

Hang in there, but don't hang out in your situation. Keep moving, and soon you will arrive at your destination.

Isaiah 43:2
When you pass through the waters, I will be with thee; and through the rivers, they shall not overflow thee: when you walk through the fire, you will not be burned; neither shall the flame kindle upon thee.

I've found that the best way to *cancel* my *burdens* is to *count* my *blessings*.

Deuteronomy 28:2
And all these blessings shall come on thee, and overtake thee, if thou shalt hearken unto the voice of the Lord thy God.

No matter how old you are, you will still be tested. However, the good news is that our Teacher only gives open Book tests.

No matter what you are going through, the answer is in the Bible. Open it up today, and you will find the answer to every problem that you can't mathematically figure out!

Don't be *mean* in the *meantime*.

> 1 Peter 5:10
> But the God of all grace, who hath called us unto his eternal glory by Christ Jesus, after that ye have suffered a while, make you perfect, stablish, strengthen, settle you.

When Jesus was an infant, His mother listened to His *cries from the cradle*.

When Jesus was thirty-three, His Father listened to His *cries from the cross*.

> Mark 15:34
> And at the ninth hour Jesus cried with a loud voice, saying, Eloi, Eloi, lama sabachthani? which is, being interpreted, My God, my God, why hast thou forsaken me?

> Luke 23:46
> And when Jesus had cried with a loud voice, he said, Father, into thy hands I commend my spirit: and having said thus, he gave up the ghost.

I think you misunderstood. Jesus said that He would give you an *abundant* life. Why have you settled for a *redundant* one?

John 10:10
The thief cometh not, but for to steal, and to kill, and to destroy: I am come that they might have life, and that they might have it more abundantly.

Ecclesiastes 2:17
Therefore I hated life; because the work that is wrought under the sun is grievous unto me: for all is vanity and vexation of spirit.

I asked someone, "How are you doing?"
They said, "Under the circumstances, I'm fine."
I said, "Why are you *under* there?"
We all have difficult circumstances, but somehow we need to learn to stand on them and not lay under them.
You can't *stand on* the promise and *lay under* the circumstance.

Don't let the impossibility of not being able to go back and *undo* keep you from the possibility of going forward and *doing*.

Philippians 3:13
Brethren, I count not myself to have apprehended: but this one thing I do, forgetting those things which are behind, and reaching forth unto those things which

are before.

Spending time in the presence of God allows God to *download in you* a higher power than the *heavy load on you.*

Matthew 11:28
Come unto me, all ye that labour and are heavy laden, and I will give you rest.

The thief comes to steal, kill, and destroy. Jesus has come to give you abundant life.

So, remember that God's *plan* for you is more prominent than satan's *plot* against you.

John 10:10
The thief comes only to steal and kill and destroy; I have come that they may have life, and have it to the full.

It's okay if your problems drive you to drink as long as you drink from the well of salvation.

Isaiah 12:3
Therefore with joy shall ye draw water out of the wells of salvation.

John 7:37
In the last day, that great day of the feast, Jesus stood and cried, saying, If any man thirst, let him come unto me, and drink.

Life is not one big *party*. It's one big *parting*.

Everyone is destined to depart from this life. Those who regularly party will likely miss the afterparty.

Psalm 16:11
Thou wilt show me the path of life: in thy presence is fulness of joy; at thy right hand there are pleasures for evermore.

I love the Moses moments in my life when God says, *"Stand still and see."*

But honestly, most of our lives are spent in days like David's, when God says, *"Be still and know."*

Exodus 14:13
And Moses said unto the people, Fear ye not, stand still, and see the salvation of the LORD, which he will

show to you to day: for the Egyptians whom ye have seen today, ye shall see them again no more for ever.

Psalm 46:10
Be still and know, that I am God: I will be exalted among the heathen, I will be exalted in the earth.

Those of us who were raised in Church well remember the little song, "This Little Light of Mine."

As a full grown adult Christian, I'm amazed at how little my light still is. I thought by now that I would be like Moses, and people would have to squint when they see me because I'm so bright.

So far, that hasn't happened.

I know I will never be as bright as the Son, but I do want to be His reflection. Maybe I can be a star and lead people to Jesus.

Most of the time though, I feel like a little night-light. I'm okay with that too because it sure is a dark world. If I can keep people from stubbing their toe when they get up at night, that's a pretty big deal. (If you've ever stubbed your toe, could I get an amen?)

Whatever light is inside of me, I won't let satan blow it out, and I won't put it under a bushel. "This little light of mine, I'm gonna let it shine."

I'm the kind of person that tries to help everybody, everywhere, every time. So it's not an excuse when I say that sometimes Jesus is the only one that can help you.

One day, eleven guys observed as Peter got out of the boat. I'm sure they applauded him when he walked on water. But when he began to sink, there was absolutely nothing they could do. They were in the middle of a storm too, and they couldn't purposely get out of their boat that seemingly would sink soon.

Peter only had one person that he could call for help. That's why he screamed. "JESUS, SAVE ME!"

Jesus did.

As "spiritual" as I am, I can't walk on water to save people who are drowning in their situations. The truth is, I can barely swim. However, the One that you were trying to get to, whenever you started going under, is right there. He's waiting to rescue you and give you another chance at life.

Anything I can do to help you, I will. But I have limits. Anything Jesus can help you with, call Him now. He has no limits!

I'll see you back in the boat!

When the strong *prey* on the weak, the weak *pray* for strength against the strong.

The *power to pray* will always be stronger than the *power to prey.*

Ezekiel 34:22
Therefore will I save my flock, and they shall no more
be a prey.

If I were to write a book about all of the things that I can't
do, it would be a hardback volume with thousands of pages of
lamentable readings.

On the other hand, if I were to write about the things that I
can do, it would not be a book. It would be a sentence.

So today I choose to write that one sentence from one of
Paul's many books.

Philippians 4:13
I can do all things through Christ who gives me
strength.

When you scream, "I CAN'T DO THIS ANYMORE," it's
not a defeat. It's an acceptance. The moment you decide you
can't do it on your own is the moment that Jesus knows He is
free to help you.

1 Corinthians 10:13
There hath no temptation taken you but such as is
common to man: but God is faithful, who will not
suffer you to be tempted above that ye are able; but
will with the temptation also make a way to escape,

that ye may be able to bear it.

The story of David and Goliath is more about *defending* God than it is *defeating* Goliath.

It is true that God is our Defender. However, as a Christian, it is our job to defend Him also. Our defending Him is as simple as taking a stand to let the world know that He is our God.

Conversely, His defense of us includes Him fighting the battles for us-sometimes through us. It is a proven fact that when you defend God, that He will defeat your enemy. When you stand for God, He will always stand with you and defeat anything that comes against you!

Whether you are lifting weights in the natural or laying aside weights in the spirit, your *greatest strength* will come through your *greatest struggle*.

Hebrews 12:1
Wherefore seeing we also are compassed about with so great a cloud of witnesses, let us lay aside every weight, and the sin which doth so easily beset us, and let us run with patience the race that is set before us,

Just because you *sailed* doesn't make you a *sailor*.

Just because you *failed* doesn't make you a *failure*.

Micah 7:8
Rejoice not against me, O mine enemy: when I fall, I shall arise; when I sit in darkness, the Lord shall be a light unto me.

You can't put a *bandage* on brokenness. It requires a *cast*.

1 Peter 5:7
Casting all your care upon him; for he cares for you.

The over *exaggerated giant* fell down as soon as the *underestimated shepherd boy* stood up.

David was a young boy who kept his Father's sheep. Goliath was a 9'6" giant who kept David's brothers in fear. When David came to bring his brothers food, he was bothered by their fear of this giant. He immediately agreed to kill the giant.

The problem was, from a natural perspective, David was no match for this monster. But, David had learned a secret: It's not the size of the man coming against you; it's the size of the God that lives in you.

Yes, that day Goliath took a tumble and lost his head, and the brothers of David and all of Israel rejoiced. So, don't let the size of your enemies fool you. It's obvious that because of God David was *underestimated* and Goliath was *over exaggerated*.

Today, it's the same for your giants. Don't over exaggerate the size of the problem nor underestimate the size of the God in you.

For dreams to abound, they can't be abandoned.

Sometimes, people who have no self-worth, self-medicate and self-inflict pain on the body that they feel is not adequate. Today, I want to remind you that one of the main attributes of Jesus was His ability to take on the inadequacy of self, by taking your feelings upon Himself. If you will obey this verse and allow Him to heal your hurt, your future self will thank you.

1 Peter 2:24
Who his own self bare our sins in his own body on the tree, that we, being dead to sins, should live unto righteousness: by whose stripes ye were healed.

You dropped the ball;
You hit the wall;
You took a fall.
Now Jesus is waiting to take your call.

In a pessimistic world, I try my best to be an optimist. However, I still have to differentiate between fantasy and reality.

The fantasy is *row, row, row your boat gently down the stream.*

The reality is *paddle, paddle, paddle your boat fiercely up the stream.*

Keep paddling. I have faith in you. You will make it!

Christianity is more like *setting your sails* than *starting your engines*. It's not how fast you start; it's about the consistency it takes to get to the other shore.

When you make statements like, *I can't believe my life turned out this way,* in reality, you are saying that you accept defeat. That is just another way of saying, *my life is over.*

If you are still breathing, your life hasn't "turned out" yet. I don't mean to be crude, but let the preacher that does the eulogy at your funeral talk about the way your life "turned out," as he speaks to all of the people that turn out to pay their respects to you.

But, it's not the time for that yet. You are not finished. Your life has not "turned out" yet. Through faith, I proclaim that things are going to take a turn for the better. It's your turn to change your turnout!

No worries! Because of the blood of Jesus, the enemy's *combat* cannot stop your *comeback*.

> Isaiah 54:17
> No weapon that is formed against thee shall prosper; and every tongue that shall rise against thee in judgment thou shalt condemn. This is the heritage of the servants of the Lord, and their righteousness is of me, saith the Lord.

Your tears are a testimony of your test. Tears water the harvest of the hope that you have planted. Psalm 126:5 says, "They that sow in tears shall reap in joy."

So, the tears you sow in the soil simply water the wonder that God is about to do in you!

Mary Magdalene was delivered of seven devils. She hung out with a lady who delivered a firstborn Son who was the Son of God.

Many years before either of those women were born, what they had in them had already met and been together. When Mary's Son talked to Mary Magdalene's devils, they recognized His voice from eternity.

Mary Magdalene was delivered from the demons by the Son that Mary delivered. Yes, the Jesus in you is stronger than the devil in others!

When asked how things are, most of us respond, "Everything is great!" Truthfully, everything usually isn't great. There are great times and great days, but very seldom is everything great at the same time.

As I pondered this thought, I was reminded of a scripture from Ecclesiastes 3:11 that says, "He has made everything beautiful in its time."

So if God makes everything beautiful in its time, everything that needs to be great in my life will be great-in its time.

Words are very powerful, so sometimes you have to change how you say something.

Maybe instead of saying, "I'm going through a trial," you could say, "I'm growing through a trial."

At the end of the day and at the end of time, it won't be what I go through; it will be what I grow through.

Don't *over-sit* when you don't *understand*.

Everyone has problems and issues with which we have to deal. I'm sure that many people are like me, When I have situations that I face, I don't air it out on social media nor talk much about it. My propensity is to sit alone and think.

But truthfully, that isn't the answer either. The Bible clearly instructs us to cast all of our cares on the Lord, for He cares for us. So, even when you don't understand, don't over-sit. God is in control of whatever you are facing!

Just after the betrayal of Judas and the denial of Peter, while on His way to the cross, Jesus made this statement in Luke 22:69, "But from now on, the Son of Man will be seated at the right hand of the mighty God."

He was assuring His disciples that He would be delivered from death.

So after the cross and the resurrection, those same disciples watched Him exit through the clouds. They had every right to believe that Jesus was seated where He said He was.

And after He sent back His Spirit at Pentecost, many people believed on Him. One believer named Stephen was appointed a deacon and was highly anointed to proclaim the Gospel.

After one of the most powerful sermons in the book of Acts, Stephen managed to enrage the religious opposition. These people were not just angered; they were murderous. They gathered together and bit Stephen with their teeth and stoned him with stones.

But in the middle of this misery, Stephen looked up and made a startling statement in Acts 7:55, "But he, being full of the Holy Ghost, looked up stedfastly into heaven, and saw the glory of God, and Jesus standing on the right hand of God."

Woe, woe, wait a minute. Didn't Jesus say that He would be seated on the right hand of God?

Yes, He did. So, what happened? Why does Stephen see Jesus standing?

All I can tell you is, even Jesus can't keep His seat when a preacher is preaching about Jesus! It was so glorious that Jesus Himself gave Stephen a standing ovation!

I have a feeling that He stands a lot, every time He hears one of us tell others about Him.

Jesus is your biggest cheerleader. Keep standing for Him as He stands with you!

Usually, in football, when you take a knee, it is a sign of a victory formation. The game is over, and you have won. I've found that this principle works excellent in real life too. Every time I take a knee, it becomes a victory formation, and I realize that because of the cross of Christ, I have already won.

A *manual* is defined as a handbook for giving instructions; how to do something using human effort, skill, power, or energy.

Emmanuel is defined as God with us.

His handbook is a Holy Book. It is also used for instructions. However, it teaches us how to live, not in our human effort, skill, power, and energy. It instructs us on how to go from *God with us* to *God in us*.

You can sit around and *regret*, or you can get up and *re-get*.

Joel 2:25
And I will restore to you the years that the locust hath eaten, the cankerworm, and the caterpiller, and the palmerworm, my great army which I sent among you.

Sometimes life can be really rough. The children of Israel hit yet another rough spot when the giant Goliath threatened to obliterate their whole nation.

But for every rough spot, there is always a way. Most every time, the way is not apparent to the natural man. Just like the story of Goliath, God has "a David" for every dilemma.

On that day long ago, God taught David an interesting concept, "Go to the brook and choose five smooth stones." The rest is history. One smooth stone took care of one rough spot.

Hey, God is no respecter of people. Today, if you will trust Him, He will supply something smooth for something rough.

For every rough spot in your story, God has a smooth stone for His glory.

There are multiple mentions of wells in the Bible. Both the Old and New Testaments have intriguing well stories.

But, out of all of those wells, a wishing well is never mentioned. God does not operate according to WISHES. He operates through DESIRE.

But understand -those coins that you were going to toss in the wishing well can be put in the offering plate, but you must put your faith in Christ.

If you desire it, you can acquire it!

The consolation of waking up on the wrong side of the bed is that Jesus never wakes up on the wrong side of the Throne.

Hebrews 12:2
Looking unto Jesus the author and finisher of our faith; who for the joy that was set before him endured the cross, despising the shame, and is set down at the right hand of the throne of God.

The consolation about *mourning* is...*morning* is coming.

Psalm 30:5
Weeping may endure for a night, but joy comes in the morning.

This morning, I couldn't get away from the word "volume." Like many other words in the English language, it has a multiplicity of meanings. Usually, when we think about volume, we think of something that needs to be turned up or turned down. This kind of volume is the perception of loudness, from the intensity of sound waves.

But then there is another volume which I deem to be a little more critical. It is a book forming part of a work or series. It can also be the amount of space that a substance or object occupies, or that is enclosed within a container, especially when the enclosed space is great.

In Psalm 40:7, the Psalmist provides a prophecy concerning Jesus. It says, "Then said I, Lo, I come: in the volume of the book it is written of me...."

In a nutshell, the volume (loudness of my life and our church services) must not be greater than the volume (the Book about Jesus and the space He occupies in our lives). When my heart is full of the volume about God, I can loudly declare with volume the greatness of God.

Turn up the volume!

The same God that shut the mouth of *lions* for Daniel shut the mouth of *liars* for Joseph.

With Christ living in you, your *inner strength* will always be greater than your *inner struggles*.

According to the Apostle Paul, God's strength is perfected by our weakness. Be strong in the Lord today!

> 2 Corinthians 12:9
> And he said unto me, My grace is sufficient for thee: for my strength is made perfect in weakness.

My email address is tommy.galloway@comcast.net. Jesus' email is JesusChrist@COMECASTyourcaresonHim.come.

Matthew 11:28
Come unto me, all ye that labour and are heavy laden, and I will give you rest.

1 Peter 5:7
Casting all your care upon him; for he careth for you.

In 1748, Benjamin Franklin wrote an article that he called "Advice to a Young Tradesman, Written by an Old One."

While the whole article is worth the read, most of us have heard one of the phrases that he coined in this publication. He said, "Time is money."

I have to agree. Every day we spend our time on whatever we choose. Since this is true, TIME has to be treated as an investment. You have to know where to deposit it to get the best return and when to withdraw.

There is a super thin line of knowing who or what is a withdrawal of your time and who or what is a deposit of your time.

When you exit this life, you may leave money for others to spend, but you will not leave one minute of time for someone else to enjoy.

Time is money. Invest it wisely.

When God doesn't give you a breakthrough, He walks through it with you.

A breakthrough is an instantaneous miracle of sorts, where something suddenly changes. I believe in those type of miracles and have experienced a few for myself.

However, a lot of life's trials and challenges are something that you have to walk through.

The key is God being with you. If you have a BREAKTHROUGH, God caused it. But, if you have a WALKTHROUGH, He was right there with you.

Either way, He gets you to the other side, right where you are supposed to be.

> Psalm 23:1-6
> The Lord is my shepherd; I shall not want. He maketh me to lie down in green pastures: he leadeth me beside the still waters. He restoreth my soul: he leadeth me in the paths of righteousness for his name's sake. Yea, though I WALK THROUGH the valley of the shadow of death, I will fear no evil: for thou art with me; thy rod and thy staff they comfort me. Thou preparest a table before me in the presence of mine enemies: thou anointest my head with oil; my cup runneth over. Surely goodness and mercy shall follow me all the days of my life: and I will dwell in the house of the Lord for ever.

Never forget 9/11 when the Towers fell.

Always remember, according to Proverbs 18:10, the name of the Lord is a strong TOWER. The righteous run into it and are safe.

Your *highest hopes* are usually not experienced until after your *deepest hurts*.

As a young man, Joseph had high hopes because of the dreams that God gave him. He lived every day of his life anticipating that *today* would be the day his dreams became reality.

Little did he know that thirteen years would roll by and tears would roll down his face before he would see his dreams fulfilled. He found out that your highest hopes are only experienced after your deepest hurts.

But the good news is, there is still hope after the hurt!

You are a limited *edition*. Stop trying to be a *rendition* of someone else!

Psalm 139:14
I will praise you; for I am fearfully and wonderfully made: marvellous are your works; and that my soul knows very well.

When someone tells you that you are not normal, take it as a compliment not as an insult.

Any ol' person can be normal, but God created you to be spectacular!

1 Peter 2:9
But ye are a chosen generation, a royal priesthood, an holy nation, a peculiar people; that ye should shew forth the praises of him who hath called you out of darkness into his marvellous light:

You don't have to flip a coin.
God has already said that you are the head and not the tail.

Deuteronomy 28:13
The Lord will make you the head, not the tail. If you pay attention to the commands of the Lord your God that I give you this day and carefully follow them, you will always be at the top, never at the bottom.

Just because you suffered a loss doesn't make you a loser.
Sometimes a loss is God's way of becoming your life preserver.

Luke 17:33
Whosoever shall seek to save his life shall lose it; and whosoever shall lose his life shall preserve it.

No matter how hard you try, you will never find the missing *pieces* of your life until you discover the missing *peace* in your life.

Try Jesus; He is the PRINCE of PEACE.

Jesus is not the missing piece in the puzzle of your life.

He is the missing *peace* in your entire life.

I just talked to the Author that wrote your life story. If you could read what He wrote, you wouldn't give up. And, yes, it ends with "happily ever after." Hang in there. Jesus is not just the Author; He is also the Finisher.

Hebrews 12:2

Looking unto Jesus the Author and Finisher of our faith; who for the joy that was set before him endured the cross, despising the shame, and is set down at the right hand of the throne of God.

Wit's end is not a dead end.

I think most have heard the term, "I'm at my wit's end." What you may or may not know is that this is a Biblical term.

Psalm 107:27
They reel to and fro, and stagger like a drunken man,
and are at their wit's end.

Wit's end is not a fun place to be. It's a place where you feel like you can't take another step or make another start. We have all been there, and many are there now. So what do we do?

Well, first of all, we have to realize that God promised that His strength would be made perfect in our weakness. He also promised for all of those things that seem to be more than we can bear that He would make a way of escape.

The way that I see it this morning is-wit's end is not a dead end. It's just a place where the familiar ends, and the new adventure begins. Sometimes a new trail will lead you to new truths.

Ultimately, when we come to the end of ourselves, we come to the beginning of the miracle that God has planned for our lives.

Never underestimate the power of something small.

One man can be a menace to millions, but one mosquito can take that mean man down.

Chapter 6
The Faithfulness of God

The Prodigal Son memorized his speech of repentance, but before he could *rehearse* it, his Father had already *reversed* it.

Sometimes the most famous speeches are those that you never have to give.

All the way from the pigpen back to the Father's house, the prodigal rehearsed what he would say to his Father.

He never got to give the speech that he had memorized. The love of the Father silenced the son's words of regret by restoring him to the reverse of what he had rehearsed.

There is no statute of limitations on the mercy of God. If you're reading this, you woke up to new mercy today. Right now, if you will pray a little prayer as simple as, "Lord have mercy," He will.

Lamentations 3:22-23
It is of the Lord's mercies that we are not consumed, because his compassions fail not. They are new every

morning: great is thy faithfulness.

Sometimes the hardest part about obeying God is not the 9' 6" giant that is staring you down. It's the average size brothers that think you are a fool for even thinking about facing that giant.

When David committed himself to God, he committed to following everything that God spoke to him. When he came to bring his brothers some cheese and crackers, he saw their dilemma and offered to be their deliverer.

However, David's oldest brother Eliab told him that he was just full of pride, that he was being naughty and only came to see the battle.

But it wasn't long until Eliab was eating his words, and the birds were eating the dead flesh of a 9'6" giant.

When you know what *God said to you*, you won't be affected by what *other people say about you*.

Most of life's *lessons* are meant to teach us to *lessen* our reliance on self and to trust in God.

John 3:30
He must increase, but I must decrease.

God is not unwilling to forgive.

Some people are just unwilling to ask.

Matthew 7:7-8

Ask, and it shall be given you; seek, and ye shall find; knock, and it shall be opened unto you.

For every one that asks receives; and he that seeks finds; and to him that knocks it shall be opened.

Isaiah 9:6 is a powerful verse about Jesus being Wonderful, Counselor, Mighty God, Everlasting Father, and Prince of Peace.

But before it says any of those things, it says "the government shall be on His shoulders."

I have great news! This government has been in operation for 2000 plus years, and it has never shut down. It's been open 24/7, 365.

And even now at 9:25 a.m. Mississippi time, Jesus is busy shouldering every need that we have.

You can always depend on the government of God!

Have you ever felt sorry for someone? You look at them in their dire situation, and there is absolutely nothing you can do except to feel so sorry for them. That is such a sad feeling of not being able to do anything to help.

However, on the other hand, all of us were in dire need. God looked at us and said, "I have to do something." So, He sent His Son, not because He felt *sorry* for us, but so He could feel *sorrow* for us!

Isaiah 53:3-4
He is despised and rejected of men; a man of sorrows, and acquainted with grief: and we hid as it were our faces from him; he was despised, and we esteemed him not.

Surely he hath borne our griefs, and carried our sorrows: yet we did esteem him stricken, smitten of God, and afflicted.

What an awesome God! I feel sorry for those that don't know He took their sorrow.

Jesus didn't just *feel sorry* for you; He *felt sorrow* for you.

God is not looking for His bride in a beauty pageant but in a pile of ashes.

His specialty is giving you beauty for ashes.

Isaiah 61:3
To appoint unto them that mourn in Zion, to give unto them beauty for ashes, the oil of joy for mourning, the garment of praise for the spirit of heaviness; that they might be called trees of righteousness, the planting of the Lord, that he might be glorified.

People promise you the moon.

God promised you the Son.
Only one fulfilled His promise.

Jesus spent three days in a *grave* so you could spend your life with *grace*.

John 2:19
Jesus answered and said unto them, destroy this temple, and in three days I will raise it up.

Titus 3:7
That being justified by his grace, we should be made heirs according to the hope of eternal life.

When Jesus came to earth, He had a huge to-do list. All through the four Gospels, as He did miracle after miracle, He would refer to that list His Father had given Him. But He continually made it very clear that His main task was not *to do*; He came *to die*.

Matthew 20:28
Even as the Son of man came not to be ministered unto, but to minister, and to give his life a ransom for many.

Rome wasn't built in a day, but it was built on ruins.

Be patient as God restores your ruins and builds you back more significant than you ever were. He is still giving beauty for ashes.

> Isaiah 61:3
> To appoint unto them that mourn in Zion, to give unto them beauty for ashes, the oil of joy for mourning, the garment of praise for the spirit of heaviness; that they might be called trees of righteousness, the planting of the Lord, that he might be glorified.

The cross was not a comfort zone. It was a place to prepare for the *Comforter* to come.

> John 14:16
> And I will pray the Father, and he shall give you another Comforter, that he may abide with you for ever;

For all who refer to God as the Man upstairs, I have some good news for you. Not only did He come downstairs and die for your sins, but He also went to the basement and took the keys of death, hell, and the grave! And, when He left and went back upstairs, He sent His Spirit back to live down in your heart. You don't have to look upstairs and scream His name;

you can whisper it because He is living just a few inches below your vocal cords.

2 Corinthians 8:9
For you know the grace of our Lord Jesus Christ, that, though he was rich, yet for your sakes he became poor, that ye through his poverty might be rich.

Ephesians 4:8-10
Wherefore he saith, when he ascended up on high, he led captivity captive, and gave gifts unto men. (Now that he ascended, what is it but that he also descended first into the lower parts of the earth? He that descended is the same also that ascended up far above all heavens, that he might fill all things.)

God's *sufficiency* meets all of my *deficiencies*.

2 Corinthians 12:9
And he said unto me, My grace is sufficient for thee: for my strength is made perfect in weakness. Most gladly therefore will I rather glory in my infirmities, that the power of Christ may rest upon me.

The bad news is, all have sinned and fallen short of the glory of God.

The good news is, what you have done has been forgiven because of what Jesus did on the cross.

Romans 3:23
For all have sinned, and come short of the glory of God;

Colossians 2:13
And you, being dead in your sins and the uncircumcision of your flesh, hath he quickened together with him, having forgiven you all trespasses; 14 Blotting out the handwriting of ordinances that was against us, which was contrary to us, and took it out of the way, nailing it to his cross;

It doesn't matter who is in your *corner* when you realize Who was on your *cross*.

The bad news is, in life, you will have tests.
The good news is, Jesus doesn't grade on the *curve*.
He gives grace from the *cross*.

There's only one thing to do when God's love *surrounds* you: *Surrender*.

Jesus stayed in Mary's womb for *9 months*. He stayed in Joseph's tomb for *3 days*. But, He committed to staying in your heart *4ever*.

Don't allow anyone to continually throw up in your face what God has thrown away by His grace.

> Psalm 103:12
> As far as the east is from the west, so far hath he removed our transgressions from us.

> Micah 7:19
> He will turn again, he will have compassion upon us; he will subdue our iniquities; and thou wilt cast all their sins into the depths of the sea.

Being burned is standard terminology for people that have been abused or misused by another person. All that remains in the aftermath of something or someone being burned is a pile of ashes. Everyone knows that there is nothing beautiful about ashes, right? The only thing positive that you can get from a pile of ashes is found in God's great exchange.

Isaiah 61:3

To appoint unto them that mourn in Zion, to give unto them beauty for ashes, the oil of joy for mourning, the garment of praise for the spirit of heaviness; that they might be called trees of righteousness, the planting of the LORD, that he might be glorified.

It's a straightforward process. You bring your ashes to Jesus, and He gives you His beauty. No questions asked.

Jesus made an *escape* so that you would not have to make an *excuse*.

Jesus had to feel God's *absence* so that you could feel His *presence*.

If you are a Christian, you know that everything that happened on the cruel cross of Calvary was for you. It's hard to pick and choose which of the brutal attacks on Jesus were worse. But seemingly, it wasn't the acts of abuse by a man that affected Jesus the most. It seems the thing that made Jesus the most miserable was feeling the absence of God. But at the end of the day, for you and me to feel God's presence, Jesus had to feel His absence.

Thank you, Jesus, for all that you did so that we can feel your presence on a daily basis!

Matthew 27:46
And about the ninth hour Jesus cried out with a loud voice, saying, "Eli, Eli, lama sabachthani?" that is, "My God, My God, why have You forsaken Me?"

Your free salvation cost Jesus more than *an arm and a leg*. It cost Him 39 stripes, a crown of thorns, a pierced side, and *His life*.

The gospels record a story of the disciples in a boat in the "eye" of a storm. They were terrified beyond measure. But Jesus came to them walking on water. He said to them, "it is *I*; be not afraid."
In the *"eye"* of the storm, Jesus is the *"I"* in the storm

The scars and stripes from a cross made it possible for the stars and stripes on a flag.

While walking this morning, I passed the BancorpSouth Arena, our city's coliseum. They have a massive billboard rented by advertisers. As I walked by this digitally enhanced sign, I saw this ad: Budweiser; Make a plan to make it home.

Now, please pay close attention as you read this post. I know that I am a Preacher, but I am not going to go into a theological exhortation of the evils of alcohol. But, I do have a message for you.

What I read into this marketing strategy is this: Budweiser wants you to spend your money and enjoy their product. But they know that if you drink too much, you lose your ability to function correctly. They want you to be thrilled, but they don't want you to be killed. This ad is designed to encourage you to get a designated driver.

As I thought about this, I could not help but think about their slogan, "Make a plan to make it home."

How do you do that? Well, it's very straightforward. God has already sent you a designated driver. Well, He wasn't a driver: He was a designated deliverer. He came to the cross with a plan to help you make it home. He was killed so you could be thrilled. I have to tell you that no matter what your addictions are, Jesus wants to you to feel what it is like to be filled with His Spirit. I promise you, if you allow yourself to be filled, you will be thrilled. It is indeed the greatest joy that you will ever experience.

So, as you get ready to celebrate this weekend of freedom, remember that your true freedom came from a designated deliverer.

He made a plan for you to make it home!

God is always working on your *behalf* for you to *be whole*.

After Jesus paid the price for your sin, He did not put you in a work-release program. He never intended for you to have to "work off" all of your evil deeds during the day and be reincarcerated at night. Calvary was God's idea of a total payment for all of your sin; therefore, His total ransom resulted in your release.

The day you realize that you can't work hard enough to pay Him back, you will start working with Him to tell other prisoners your story of His great release.

You often hear people talk about the *splendor* of the King.

Wow, what splendor He offers! However, the splendor could not have happened without the *splinters* (thorns).

Interestingly, the original curse in Eden for Adam had to do with *thorns*. I find it so amazing that Jesus was crowned with the curse of the original sin. That day at Calvary, He broke every curse by breaking the original one!

The devil tries to use permanent markers to mark your life. Once the ink dries on your failures, he wants you to feel finished, displaying your sin stains for life. He hopes you never find out about the blood of Calvary.

It is proven that the blood of the spotless Lamb of God is the only thing that can permanently wash away what the devil thought was a permanent mark.

I *figuratively* said to the Lord, "I have the weight of the world on my shoulders."

The Lord said back to me, "I *literally* know how you feel."

Three *rusty nails* held Jesus to the cross just long enough to prove that He loves you with *no strings attached*.

Jesus put Himself in the *crossfire* for your soul.

He went to the *cross* so you wouldn't go to the *fire*.

Jesus had a pre-existing condition.

He was the Lamb slain from the foundation of the world. Thankfully, His Father had a great *life assurance* policy, of which you and I are the beneficiaries.

God doesn't suffer from memory loss, yet He can't remember your past.

We suffer from future loss because we do.

Jesus went through a very *complicated* process to bring you the *simplicity* of salvation.

Jesus didn't put you on His *to-do* list.
He put you on His *to-die-for* list.

Old folks play records.
Athletes set records.
Other people break their records.
Analysts keep up with records.
But thankfully, God doesn't keep records.
Your sins are forgiven. There's no record of them anywhere!

As humans, there are four words that we should take out of our vocabulary because they're words that can never happen. Those four words are: If I were you.

You will never be me, and I will never be you. Therefore, I have no clue what I would do if I were you, and you have no inkling as to what you would do if you were in my shoes. Yes, it's humanly impossible for us to be each other.

But, if you were God…

God said, "If I were you," and then He thought, *I can be you. I will be you. I am you.*

Hebrews 7:26
For such an high priest became us, who is holy, harmless, undefiled, separate from sinners, and made

higher than the heavens;

You can say, "Lord, have mercy," and know He does.
You can say, "People, have mercy," and hope they will.

The study of our DNA is amazing. But now there is a new study called epigenetics, and it is believed through this process that your genes can be altered.

While this is somewhat good news, there has been a similar plan in place since long ago.

People blame their genetics on everything from what they eat to what they drink to how much or how little they exercise, and even to their horrible habits.

I know I'm a little "old school," but I believe that when an individual has the blood of Calvary applied to his/her life, it alters everything.

Therefore, I believe that every generational curse stops at the cross, as well as any lifestyle change that needs to be appropriated to your life.

The bottom line is, you can spend money on science and have your genes altered, or you can go to the altar of God, claim Calvary's blood, and get it done for free.

When God reigns, He pours!

Joel 2:28
And it shall come to pass afterward, that I will pour out my spirit upon all flesh; and your sons and your daughters shall prophesy, your old men shall dream dreams, your young men shall see visions:

People give you a *grade* on your *performance*. God gives you *grace* when you don't *perform* very well. People will fail you, but God never will.

I'll never get *over the grace* that Jesus brought when He was born *under the Law*.

Titus 2:11
For the grace of God that brings salvation hath appeared to all men,

Galatians 4:4
But when the fullness of the time was come, God sent forth his Son, made of a woman, made under the law,

Jesus didn't just cross His fingers and wish for the best. He went to a cross and gave His all.

Jesus didn't just walk out of a tomb where others placed him; He walks through walls into rooms where you have placed yourself.

John 20:19
Then the same day at evening, being the first day of the week, when the doors were shut where the disciples were assembled for fear of the Jews, came Jesus and stood in the midst, and saith unto them, Peace be unto you.

Most of the time, when people exclaim, "I don't deserve this," it's because something negative has happened to them.

But this phrase needs to be used because something positive has happened to you. After examining the Mercy of God, all of us can truthfully exclaim, "I don't deserve this!"

The longest text message ever recorded is 774,746 words. It's called the Bible. God doesn't expect you to *reply* to His text in writing, but He does expect you to *comply* in living.

Whatever you are going through, Jesus went through it too. And, *He nailed it*!

Hebrews 4:15
For we have not an high priest which cannot be touched with the feeling of our infirmities; but was in all points tempted like as we are, yet without sin.

Colossians 2:14
Blotting out the handwriting of ordinances that was against us, which was contrary to us, and took it out of the way, nailing it to his cross.

When Jesus went to the country of the Gadarenes, He had a purpose. There was a man there that was demon possessed. As Jesus approached this desperate soul, the demons identified themselves as Legion, which means *many*.

Of course, many demons have never bothered Jesus. He can cast out one or millions with His pinky. But my intention is not to talk about the man's past. I don't want to emphasize what he was, but who he became.

Yes, Jesus is the only One that can deliver you from a *legion* and make you a *legend*!

Jesus said, "I am the Way."

The writer of Hebrews tells us that Jesus went out of His way to go to the cross.

There's nothing like *The Way* going *out of His way* to make *a way* for us!

John 14:6
Jesus saith unto him, I am the way, the truth, and the life: no man cometh unto the Father, but by me.

Colossians 2:14
Blotting out the handwriting of ordinances that was against us, which was contrary to us, and took it out of the way, nailing it to his cross;

Every time I tell the Lord how *deficient* I am, He tells me how *sufficient* He is.

2 Corinthians 12:9
And he said unto me, My grace is sufficient for you: for my strength is made perfect in weakness.

God is the only one that can make your *hope* bigger than your *hurt*.

The only way that humans could ever be holy was for a Holy God to become a human.

2 Corinthians 8:9
For ye know the grace of our Lord Jesus Christ, that, though he was rich, yet for your sakes he became poor, that ye through his poverty might be rich.

Hebrews 7:26
For such an high priest became us, who is holy, harmless, undefiled, separate from sinners, and made higher than the heavens;

Calvary had side effects. When they thrust a spear in Jesus's side, **blood** and **water** came out.

Amazingly, those were the exact two things that He chose to use in order to give us deliverance.

John 19:34
But one of the soldiers with a spear pierced his side, and forthwith came there out blood and water.

Grace doesn't measure *how bad* you have been. It measures *how good* God *is*.

John was not a Jr.

When Zacharias was performing his priestly duties in the Temple, he received a visit from the Angel Gabriel.

Gabriel surprised him with quite an interesting announcement for a man his age. He told him that his wife Elisabeth was going to have a baby and that he was to name him John.

While there are so many "fun facts" surrounding this announcement, I will cut to the chase. Just like Gabriel said, Elisabeth had a bouncing baby boy. He was welcomed by tons of kinfolks that rejoiced with Zacharias and Elisabeth.

But when it came time to name the baby, everyone thought that his name should be Zacharias, Jr. But both parents defied what the kinfolks suggested because God said to call him John.

Therefore John was not a Jr.!

Too many Christians are trying to live a "Jr." relationship. They feel that they have inherited enough Christianity from their family. However, you cannot have a Jesus Jr. mentality. You must have a personal relationship with Him.

You have been given a name that's above every name. Be sure that other people know to call you what Jesus said you would be called!

People who still *live* under the Law have trouble knowing how to *love* under Grace.

Christianity is not about *enforcing* laws; it's about *endorsing* grace.

Conversations about Christ are good.
Conversions to Christ are wonderful.

Jesus is the only Man that ever lived that didn't have a skeleton in His *closet*.

He's also the only Man that ever died that doesn't have a skeleton in His *coffin*.

Joseph was placed in the pit by his brothers who lied to their Father about what happened. He was sold as a slave to Potiphar, then lied on by Potiphar's wife when he refused her advances. These lies caused him to be cast in prison, but he was not cast down in spirit. Joseph knew what you need to learn.

The *truth* will always be *validated* no matter what *lie* has been *fabricated*!

You can only tell your *rags to riches* story because Jesus had a *riches to rags* story.

  2 Corinthians 8:9
  For ye know the grace of our Lord Jesus Christ, that,
  though he was rich, yet for your sakes he became

poor, that ye through his poverty might be rich.

If you are the bride of Christ, you never have to worry about Jesus leaving you at the altar.

Ever so often you get the sad news that someone didn't show up for their own wedding. The term for that is "left at the altar." Even though it's rare, it does happen once in a blue moon at weddings.

But sadly, it happens almost every Sunday to Jesus. People come to church, pray, ask Jesus for His help, and then they "leave Him at the altar."

An altar was never made for someone to be left at, but as a place to meet God and take Him with you!

Jesus did not put His grace on a lay-a-way plan. You can't pay a little here, a little there, and get Him out when you've paid the quota. He paid the price in full at Calvary.

Your debt is paid. Enjoy the gift!

There's an adage that says, "It will all come out in the wash." That means to not worry about adverse situations, because in the end, it will all come out okay. I'm so glad that applies to my sins also.

If you have asked Jesus to forgive you, it will all come out in the wash!

Revelation 1:5
...Jesus Christ loved us, and washed us from our sins
in his own blood.

Calvary wasn't a *risk*; it was a *rescue*.

In a world where the media skews the news, I'm glad I have
a Bible that is reliable. The Bible is still GOOD NEWS!

Jesus is tougher than nails!

Colossians 2:14
Blotting out the handwriting of ordinances that was
against us, which was contrary to us, and took it out
of the way, nailing it to his cross;

The Bible states that God is an ever-present help in the time
of trouble. However, there are times that we all wonder where
He is and why He's not answering.

Don't feel guilty for those feelings. Even Jesus felt that way
on the cross. With excruciating pain, He cried, "My God, My
God, why have you forsaken me?"

We know how that all turned out. He was forsaken so we could be forgiven.

Jesus had to feel the *absence* of God for you to be able to feel His *presence*.

Yes, it's true that we will have to deal with obstacles in life. However, we have to be sensitive enough to know that the bridges that Jesus crossed for us at the cross never have to be crossed again!

The cross will help you to cross any barrier.

God said, *"Let there be,"* not *"Let me see."*

God doesn't have to think about what He has already promised you that He will do.

When God cleans your heart, He clears your history.

Because of what the devil did in a tree and what Eve did from a tree, Christ had to be hung on a tree.

Genesis 3:1-6
Now the serpent was more subtil than any beast of the field which the Lord God had made. And he said unto the woman, Yea, hath God said, Ye shall not

eat of every tree of the garden? And the woman said unto the serpent, We may eat of the fruit of the trees of the garden: But of the fruit of the tree which is in the midst of the garden, God hath said, Ye shall not eat of it, neither shall ye touch it, lest ye die. And the serpent said unto the woman, Ye shall not surely die: For God doth know that in the day ye eat thereof, then your eyes shall be opened, and ye shall be as gods, knowing good and evil. And when the woman saw that the tree was good for food, and that it was pleasant to the eyes, and a tree to be desired to make one wise, she took of the fruit thereof, and did eat, and gave also unto her husband with her; and he did eat.

Acts 10:39
And we are witnesses of all things which he did both in the land of the Jews, and in Jerusalem; whom they slew and hanged on a tree:

When a Hockey player gets a penalty, they put him in a box. For the penalty of our sin, they put Jesus on a cross.

Colossians 2:14
Blotting out the handwriting of ordinances that was against us, which was contrary to us, and took it out of the way, nailing it to his cross.

At Calvary, the blue bruises and red blood revealed Jesus's true colors.

Isaiah 53:4-5
Surely he hath borne our griefs, and carried our sorrows: yet we did esteem him stricken, smitten of God, and afflicted. But he was wounded for our transgressions, he was bruised for our iniquities: the chastisement of our peace was upon him; and with his stripes we are healed.

Jesus said that He is the root and offspring of David. When you have the *root rooting* for you, you have no choice but to win.

Hebrews 7:25
Wherefore he is able also to save them to the uttermost that come unto God by him, seeing he ever liveth to make intercession for them.

Romans 8:31
What shall we then say to these things? If God be for us, who can be against us?

God doesn't do *heart bypasses*; He does *heart transplants*.

Ezekiel 36:26
A new heart also will I give you, and a new spirit will
I put within you: and I will take away the stony heart
out of your flesh, and I will give you an heart of flesh.

1 Samuel 10:9
And it was so, that when he had turned his back to go
from Samuel, God gave him another heart: and all
those signs came to pass that day.

In most everything that I have accomplished, the odds have
been against me.

But in everything that I have accomplished, God has
been for me.

It doesn't matter how many *odds* are *against* you; *God*
is *for* you!

Romans 8:31
What shall we then say to these things? If God be for
us, who can be against us?

God has many excellent attributes, but I find His ability
to remember and forget to be especially intriguing. He is not
unrighteous to forget our work and labor of love, but He is also
not unrighteous to remember our sins!

Hebrews 6:10
For God is not unrighteous to forget your work and labour of love, which ye have shewed toward his name, in that ye have ministered to the saints, and do minister.

Hebrews 8:12
For I will be merciful to their unrighteousness, and their sins and their iniquities will I remember no more.

To say that God is an Artist is an understatement. Out of all of His attributes, this is just one of His majestic qualities of magnificence.

The Psalmist said the heavens declare the glory of God and the firmament shows His handiwork. But God the Artist doesn't just draw scenery; He draws sinners.

Jesus said, "If I am lifted from the earth, I will draw all men to me." But it's not a brush in His hand that He will use to draw you; He draws with nails.

God doesn't want you to give Him your *best shot*. He wants your worst *shortcoming*.

God doesn't have a different wash cycle for different loads of sin.

It all has to be washed in the blood of the Lamb.

> Revelation 1:5
> ...Unto him that loved us, and washed us from our sins
> in his own blood.

Parent: Make your bed.
Critic: If you make your bed hard, you'll sleep on it.
God: If you make your bed in hell, I will still be with you.

> Psalm 139:8
> If I ascend up into heaven, you are there: if I make my
> bed in hell, behold, you are there.

People give you a grade on your performance.
God gives you grace when you didn't perform very well.
People will fail you, but God never will.

God is not a magician that makes chaos disappear.
He is the Master that makes calm appear in the
middle of chaos.

While the gamblers at Golgotha were gambling to see who could have Jesus's garments, Jesus was purchasing you and me garments of salvation and a robe of righteousness.

Mark 15:24
And when they had crucified him, they parted his garments, casting lots upon them, what every man should take.

Isaiah 61:10
I will greatly rejoice in the Lord, my soul shall be joyful in my God; for he has clothed me with the garments of salvation, he has covered me with the robe of righteousness, as a bridegroom decks himself with ornaments, and as a bride adorns herself with her jewels.

God will always take you back, but He really wants to take you forward.

Chapter 7
Inspirational Incidentals

I was reminded today of Joseph.

When he interpreted the dreams of the baker and the butler, he just knew that Pharaoh would hear of him and set him free. I'm sure that he had a mindset of: today is my day of deliverance.

But, as humans do, the butler and the baker got their prayer interpreted and answered, and they forget about the person that helped them. Yes, the Butler forgot about the man that interpreted the dream that got him delivered.

So, the day that Joseph thought would be his day of freedom turned into another day and then another. In fact, it turned into 730 more days in prison. Then at the end of two full years, Pharaoh dreamed a dream, and the butler remembered Joseph.

That was his day of freedom.

His sentence was now over, and Pharaoh made a statement that would change his life forever.

That was the end of his drama and the beginning of his dream.

Don't give up your dream. God remembers where you are, and He has a set time for your deliverance. If you spend today worrying about tomorrow, you will spend tomorrow worrying about why you worried yesterday, because what you worried about yesterday didn't happen today.

Philippians 4:6
Do not be anxious about anything, but in every situation, by prayer and petition, with thanksgiving, present your requests to God.

You will only find the *blueprint* for your life in the *nail prints* of Jesus.

Zechariah 13:6
And one shall say unto him, What are these wounds in thine hands? Then he shall answer, Those with which I was wounded in the house of my friends.

Because Jesus was God's only *Begotten* Son, you never have to worry about being God's only *forgotten* son.

John 3:16
For God so loved the world, that he gave his only begotten Son, that whosoever believes in him should

not perish, but have everlasting life.

Isaiah 49:15
Can a woman forget her nursing child, And not have compassion on the son of her womb? Surely they may forget, Yet I will not forget you.

Second only to John 3:16 in popularity is Psalm 23.

This beautiful Psalm has captured the hearts of believers and non-believers alike.

However, like many other powerful passages of scripture, most people only use one verse. It's this verse that they want to be used at funerals as solace for the valley that they are walking through. And my, how powerful it is!

Psalm 23:4 says, "Yea though I walk through the valley of the shadow of death, I will fear no evil for you are with me."

But out of all due respect, this chapter wasn't meant only to be used at a funeral. It was meant for our everyday walk with the Lord. If you take the time to read it slowly, you will find out that walking through a valley is just one of the things that you will go through.

Look at the other things:

He makes me lie down in green pastures.

He leads me beside the still waters.

He restores my soul.

He leads me in the path of righteousness.

His rod and staff comfort me.

He prepares a table before me in the presence of my enemies.

He anoints my head with oil.

My cup runs over.

Goodness and mercy are following me, all the days of my life.

Notice verse 6 says, "...all the days of my life!" Go ahead and read this at a funeral, but enjoy all of these other benefits all the days of your life and dwell in the house of the Lord forever!

"Put on the map" is a phrase that means to make someone famous, well known, or popular.

While I don't consider myself to be any of that, God has put me on the map. He has put me places that Siri can't find, but God knows where I am.

Psalm 139 gives us four places on the map that seem unlikely for anyone to ever be able to know where we are, but God knows!

1. If I ascend into heaven, He is there.
2. If I make my bed in hell, He is there.
3. If I take the wings of the morning and dwell in the uttermost parts of the sea, He is there.
4. If I hide in darkness, the night becomes light, because He is there!

Indeed, my friend, God has put you on the map. He may be the only one that knows where you are, but I assure you that His eye knows every detail of your journey.

In all of those unlikely places, He has destined you with a Heavenly destination. Soon, you will be at the place where He has for your life.

Some things in life have to be endured, but now, it is time to enjoy!

Because of hurtful things in the past, many people develop a "because of" mentality. That mentality, in turn, breeds a "what if" mentality about their future.

Because of what happened, I will never trust again, because *what if* it happens again?

But through faith in Christ, we can take one word from each phrase. Our entire life can change into "because of what."

Because of what the Lord has done for me, I never have to blame my failures on *because of*, and I never have to worry about the future *what if*.

1 John 4:19
We love Him because He first loved us.

The fact that David could kill Goliath was viewed by his brothers as a "figment of his imagination."

But after the thunderous thud of a giant on the ground, his brothers enjoyed the transformation of little brother's imagination.

People will only be skeptics and critics until they see God do through you what He has already done to you.

The only way to get *over the shame* is to get *under the shadow*.

Psalm 36:7
How excellent is thy lovingkindness, O God! therefore the children of men put their trust under the shadow of thy wings.

Romans 8:1
There is therefore now no condemnation to them which are in Christ Jesus, who walk not after the flesh, but after the Spirit.

If you are a *man*, you are not *junk male*, so you do not need a *stamp of approval*.

There is no greater joy than *one* battle down and *won* victory to go.

2 Chronicles 20:30
So the realm of Jehoshaphat was quiet: for his God gave him rest round about.

He who *sees* the day early with prayer will *seize* the day later with power.

Psalm 5:3
My voice shalt thou hear in the morning, O Lord; in the morning will I direct my prayer unto thee, and will look up.

2 Thessalonians 1:11
So we keep on praying for you, asking our God to enable you to live a life worthy of his call. May he give you the power to accomplish all the good things your faith prompts you to do.

The only way to have a *marvelous life* is to walk into God's *marvelous light*.

1 Peter 2:9
But ye are a chosen generation, a royal priesthood, an holy nation, a peculiar people; that ye should shew forth the praises of him who hath called you out of darkness into his marvellous light:

I'm honored that God has allowed me to take Him at *faith value*!

Not only was faith one of Jesus's favorite words, but it's also in every New Testament book except for three.

Most Christians can readily tell you the definition of what faith is according to Hebrews 11:1, "Now faith is, the substance of things hoped for and the evidence of things not seen."

But this morning I read this verse in 1 Peter: 8, and it ministered to me, "Though you have not seen him, you love him; and even though you do not see him now, you believe in him and are filled with an inexpressible and glorious joy."

Today, remember that even though you cannot see Him, you can still believe in Him. And because of that, your faith has filled you with unspeakable joy.

There's a super thin line between knowing too much about a situation and not knowing enough.

When you know too much, you tend to worry about what you know, but when you don't know enough, you tend to worry about what you don't know.

At times like these, the one thing you do need to know is the Word of God.

Philippians 4:6 says, "Do not be anxious about anything, but in every situation, by prayer and petition, with thanksgiving, present your requests to God."

When you know the Word, you know that the Lord has control of both the known and the unknown.

Thou shalt not *steal*.
Thou shalt be *still*.

Psalm 46:10
Be still, and know that I am God.

Jeremiah 29:11 is one of the most quoted, encouraging verses in the Bible. It says, "For I know the plans I have for you, declares the Lord. Plans to prosper you and not to harm you plans to give you hope and a future."

There is no doubt that God has great plans for all of our lives. But sometimes it seems that those plans are far in the distance. What can we do to see those plans come to fruition?

We have to get in the right place.

When Moses was asking God about His plans for his life, God said to him in Exodus 33:21, "Behold, there is a place by Me, and you shall stand upon a rock."

When Moses got to the right place, God revealed His plans in a clear, distinct manner.

I have observed countless people quoting God's plan for their life, but they have no idea of their place.

Today, the Lord is whispering to you (maybe through this post) to drop what you're doing and find a place to be alone with Him. I promise you that when you put yourself in a place close to God, His plans that have seemed concealed will be revealed!

Your *soul* motivation should be your *sole* motivation.

1 Peter 4:19
Wherefore let them that suffer according to the will of
God commit the keeping of their souls to him in well

doing, as unto a faithful Creator.

Philippians 3:13
Brethren, I count not myself to have apprehended: but this one thing I do, forgetting those things which are behind, and reaching forth unto those things which are before,

As a carpenter, Jesus *used a ruler*.
As King, *He is the Ruler*.

You don't have to cross your fingers and hope. You can look at the cross and know.

Some people think the devil knows everything that they think. No, he doesn't. He only knows *what* you do. He watches what you watch, listens to your conversations, and sees how you respond to people. All of his "temptations" come from his observations of what you do, not an omniscient knowledge that he does not possess. God is Omniscient, but the devil is not!

"I pledge allegiance to the Flag of the United States of America, and to the Republic for which it stands, one nation under God, indivisible, with liberty and justice for all."

The first three words of this historical document hold the key to where we are as a society.

As an American, it deeply bothers me that people will not pledge allegiance to the flag. However, this refusal to say the Pledge is a broader symbol of our society. Very few people will pledge allegiance to anything, much less our flag.

A pledge is defined as a solemn promise or undertaking. Allegiance is defined as loyalty, faithfulness, or devotion.

The sacredness of making a pledge to God, to Church, or to superiors is waning more and more as time progresses. And, without a pledge, there is no allegiance or loyalty to anything or anyone.

But those of us who still "hold these truths," must hold them with conviction. My pledge of allegiance, first of all to my God, then to my leaders (both spiritual and natural), and to our country, cannot be shaken by people who refuse to pledge allegiance.

At the end of the day, a pledge is who you are not what you do.

A sign of a healthy Church is whether you have more *new creatures* than you have *old critics*.

Activating your faith *deactivates* your fear.

Checklist for a Real Life *Hero*:
HE ROSE from the dead.

It looks like there is only One.

You don't have to go through every door that presents itself in front of you. But remember, your destiny *hinges* on the *door* that you choose.

Doors are everywhere. No matter what business or entity or home that you go to today, you will have to go through a door. That door you walk through has hinges holding it in place and making it possible for the door to be there.

But, it's not the hinges on the door that concern me. It's the possibility that the rest of your life will hinge on the door you walk through today.

Just remember, Jesus said, "I am The Door." If you walk with Him, He will make sure that you choose every other door correctly.

Your *strengths* do not *qualify* you to be used of God. Neither do your *weaknesses nullify* you from being used by Him.

If you are *defined* by faith, you will never be *defied* by fear.

The irony of the Christian faith is that people *stay* where God *moves*.

The church service should never be about *charming* you on Sunday. It should be about *changing* you for Monday.

Most of the people that use the term, "I wish things were the way they used to be," are the same people that were previously saying, "I wish things would hurry up and change."

You can't treat every problem the same. It's impossible to get rid of everything that bugs you.

If you have bugs bugging you, call the exterminator. He will spray poison on those pests, and they will die.

But, if you have people bugging you, you don't call the exterminator to spray and poison those people who pester you. You call Jesus and pray.

I'm not going to guarantee you that prayer will make them go away, but it will help you learn to handle people that don't do things to please you.

Jesus taught much about praying for those annoying people that don't do things right by my standards.

Pick a person today that bugs you and pray for them. It's highly possible that you will pray for me.

I believe in any program that will help people with sobriety. However, you can step into any program and follow all of their steps and still not stop your addictions. But, there is a place that's not a program with a 100% success ratio.

I don't know how many steps that Jesus walked from Gethsemane to Golgotha, but those steps have stopped millions of addictions. When Jesus stepped out of the judgment hall and headed to the cross, with every step and every stripe, your addictions were stopped by His afflictions.

On the cross, He took your curse and broke every chain that has you imprisoned by your addiction of choice.

What do you have to do?

It's a one-step plan. Step up to the cross and ask Jesus to help you.

Not only will that one step stop your addiction, but it will also start you on the path of abundant life. Forgiveness equals freedom.

Would you take that one step?

When your past imprisons you, you are the judge and the jury. You have the full right and responsibility to let yourself go. The same key that will free you from your past will unlock your future.

Why settle for seeing the Seven Wonders of the World, when you have access to thousands of wonders of the Word?

To be God's *masterpiece*, you have to be willing to give the *Master* every *piece* of you.

It doesn't matter if all of the pieces are fragmented. He needs everything that you have left.

You are more likely to fall at the place you are than things are likely to fall in place.

God did not design your life for things to fall in place. He designed you to fall in love with Him.

When you love Him, you will walk with Him. When you walk with Him, you will get to a place by walking with Him that you could not fall into automatically.

God told Moses, "There is a place by Me, and you shall stand upon a rock."

Moses didn't fall on the rock. He walked to it. And once he got to where God wanted him to be, he saw what he had been praying for come to pass.

Could I encourage you today to stop waiting for things to fall in place, and start walking to the place God has called you to be?

I'm not a proponent of the word "suck." It just sounds a little disrespectful to me. However, people use it on a daily basis to describe their condition. I often hear, "My life sucks."

Why don't you turn the negative button off and realize that the first part of success is "suc."

Suck it up and finish what you started. Turn "suc" into success.

Jesus specializes in ruining bad reputations.

A true friend is someone that will not believe something negative about you unless they hear it from you. And if they hear it from you, they still won't tell others about you.

Jesus never promised you a *knight in shining armor*. He promised that He would be your *armor and shine in your darkest night*.

> 1 Thessalonians 5:5
> Ye are all the children of light, and the children of the day: we are not of the night, nor of darkness.

Have you ever had to reintroduce yourself to yourself?

In a world where people constantly try to get you to conform to a new fad or fashion, or even a new way of thinking, sometimes it's difficult to stay true to who you are.

Peer pressure doesn't end when you graduate from high school. It's a constant tug of war that you have to deal with until you know who you are.

While people try to get you to be like them, Christ beckons you to be like Him. When you know who you are in Christ, you will constantly strive to be transformed by Him instead of being conformed to be like them.

Today would be a great day to reintroduce you to the you that God called you to be.

> Romans 12:1-2
> I beseech you therefore, brethren, by the mercies of God, that ye present your bodies a living sacrifice, holy, acceptable unto God, which is your reasonable service. And be not conformed to this world: but be ye transformed by the renewing of your mind, that ye may prove what is that good, and acceptable, and perfect, will of God.

There's no need to come to Church and *mask* your *pressures* when you can come and *bask* in God's *presence*.

> Psalm 16:11
> Thou wilt shew me the path of life: in thy presence is fulness of joy; at thy right hand there are pleasures for evermore.

What's right with God will change what's wrong with you.

It has been said that time is money. That's why the phrase "spend time" was coined.

Certainly, everyone does not have the same amount of money, and because of the uncertainty of time, no one knows really how much of that they have either. So, time should be regarded as more precious than money is guarded.

All of us have to choose where to invest our time and who to invest it in. Every minute is a deposit into or a withdrawal from your time bank.

Spend money on things you need, but spend time with those you love.

(Thanks for taking the time to read what I took the time to write. I hope this was a wise investment of your time.)

The people that love Christ's *appearing* will also love *disappearing* with Him!

> 2 Timothy 4:8
> Henceforth there is laid up for me a crown of righteousness, which the Lord, the righteous judge, shall give me at that day: and not to me only, but unto all them also that love his appearing.

Signs on Earth always follow *sounds* from Heaven.

Just before Jesus began His ministry, He was baptized by John. At His baptism, a voice boomed from Heaven validating

Him as the Son of God. After that sound from Heaven, Jesus did ministry for 3.5 years, with signs following.

At the end of His ministry, He looked at His disciples and said, "These signs shall follow them that believe." Then He instructed them to go to an upper room to be endued with power from on High. As they assembled there, they heard a sound from Heaven as a mighty rushing wind. After that sound, the Church was born, and signs were everywhere.

God is still doing signs in the earth now, but they only work after sounds from Heaven!

Christianity is having an *unshakable* faith even when you don't have an *unbreakable* heart.

A caring Christian is someone who will *pray* for you to be blessed without having to *pry* into your business.

I heard a preacher say today that God wants all Christians to be millionaires. While I'm not opposed to that, all I can find scripturally is this:

> Romans 8:17
> And if children, then heirs; heirs of God, and joint-heirs with Christ; if so be that we suffer with him, that

we may be also glorified together.

I am an heir of God and joint-heir with Christ.

Whether or not He ever allows me to have a *million dollars*, I have more than a *million reasons* to serve Him all the days of my life!

People spend hours at the gym exercising. Kudos! That's awesome.

But when was the last time that you gave your senses a workout? God promises that by reason of use, your senses will be exercised.

If you find yourself in a place where life doesn't make sense, take all five of your senses to God's gym.

On the first machine, you can work two senses at the same time. Oh, *taste* and *see* that the Lord is good.

Then you can go and *touch* the hem of the Lord's garment.

Afterward, like Noah after the flood, you can build an altar and offer God the savor of a *sweet-smelling* sacrifice.

Then, you can finish with *listening* intently to the Word of God and *hear* what the Spirit is speaking to you.

After this process, life will make more sense, because your senses are exercised!

(This may not burn any calories, but it will sure help you cast off your cares.)

Hebrews 5:14

But strong meat belongs to them that are of full age, even those who by reason of use have their *senses exercised* to discern both good and evil.

As Jesus hung on the cross, Pilate wrote a sign that read, *Jesus, King of the Jews.* Because there were people at the cross from other nations, he wrote it in Hebrew, Greek, and Latin.

When the people read it they said, "Don't write *Jesus King of the Jews;* write that He said, 'I am the King of the Jews'".

Pilate said, "What I have written I have written."

No matter how much they shouted, "Not my King, not my King," there was absolutely nothing they could do to change what the Governor and Jesus said.

Jesus was and is King. In fact, He is the King of Kings and Lord of Lords!

> John 19:19-22
> And Pilate wrote a title, and put it on the cross. And the writing was, Jesus of Nazareth, King of the Jews. This title then read many of the Jews: for the place where Jesus was crucified was nigh to the city: and it was written in Hebrew, and Greek, and Latin. Then said the chief priests of the Jews to Pilate, Write not, The King of the Jews; but that he said, I am King of the Jews. Pilate answered, What I have written I have written.

Sometimes I cry, not because something is wrong with me but because something is right with my soul.

Jesus said, "I am the Way, the Truth and the Life."

If you need satisfaction, try the Tree of Life.

If you need direction, try the Path of Life,

Which will lead you to the Way of Life.

If you are hungry, try the Bread of Life.

If you are thirsty, try the Water of Life.

If you are tired of your old life, try Newness of Life.

If something in you has died, try the Resurrection and the Life.

If you are looking for a Church, try Word of Life!

At Word of Life, we believe that Jesus is all of the things mentioned above. We preach and teach these things as well as many others, directly from the Word of God.

Our goal at Word of Life is for you to have your name written in the Lamb's Book of Life and receive the Crown of Life!

Now, that's real life. Abundant life!

For Jonah, God prepared a great fish.

For the disciples, He prepared cooked fish.

Jonah 1:17

Now the Lord had prepared a great fish to swallow up Jonah. And Jonah was in the belly of the fish three days and three nights.

John 21:9
As soon then as they were come to land, they saw a
fire of coals there, and fish laid thereon, and bread.

When you are in a natural storm, meteorologists tell you
to find your safe place. That place is usually the lowest part of
your house.

When you are in a spiritual storm, the Master also tells you
to find your safe place. That place is usually the highest part
of His Tower.

Proverbs 18:10
The name of the Lord is a strong tower: the righteous
runs into it, and is safe.

As an "old school" advocate of the Holy Scriptures, I
believe that the Bible is error-free.

However, I confess that without proper knowledge of how
to study God's Word, some things can seem a bit contradictory.
Such is the case in the following verses.

In Matthew 7:1, Jesus said, "Judge not, that ye be not judged."

Then in 1 Corinthians 6:2, Paul said, "Do you not know that
the saints shall judge the world?"

Why would Jesus say to judge not and Paul say that the saints shall judge?

Notice, Paul used the term *shall judge*. Shall is futuristic. In this instance, it speaks of the end of time after the Lord has said to His saints, "Well done." And at that point, we, as the children of God, *shall* rule and reign with Christ.

But without getting too deep into Bible prophecy or a theological debate on salvation, I merely want to make a point. As Christians, we are not to judge each other now, lest we also be judged.

Jesus said those exact words. So, that makes me wonder how the saints shall judge the world in the end, if we keep judging each other now. Won't our judgment keep us from being a saint?

It seems to me that not judging now is a prerequisite of being able to judge then.

This is just my thoughts. I'm not judging you.

When a Christian dies, the Coroner *pronounces* them *dead*, but Jesus *announces* them *alive* for evermore.

There is an adage that says, "Sticks and stones may break my bones, but words can never harm me."

Oh, how I wish that were in the Bible. If it were, I would make myself believe it. But, it's not in the Bible, and unquestionably, it is a quote that leaves us in a quandary. It's just not true.

In reality, words are worse than weapons. While weapons have the potential to kill you, words have the potential to wound you while you live. He said, she said, and they said can be ammunition that pierces the heart and causes shrapnel fragments to scatter throughout your body, soul, and spirit. Words can also be a poison that will position you not to trust anyone. The truth is, words can hurt deeply.

No, the Bible doesn't say that words will never harm you. But it does tell those of us who are Christians to choose our words carefully. In fact, it says that if you offend a little child with your words or actions that you will face the consequences. These kind of wounds are an offense against God Himself.

I know that we have all felt the wound of words, and I'm also sure that all of us can say that at some point we have wounded someone with words. But today is a new day. My prayer for me today is this Psalm. If you want it to be your prayer too, please pray it with me.

> Psalm 19:14
> Let the words of my mouth, and the meditation of my heart, be acceptable in thy sight, O LORD, my strength, and my redeemer.

I know the Bible says that we have this treasure in an earthen vessel. Without a doubt, God has deposited His Spirit in us. However, God never intended for us to be a safe deposit box. He wants others to be able to "bank on" the Spirit flowing freely from our lives.

2 Corinthians 4:7

But we have this treasure in earthen vessels, that the excellency of the power may be of God, and not of us.

The Apostle Paul found himself imprisoned frequently. As he was writing the book of Ephesians from a Roman jail, he made a startling statement in Ephesians 3:1. He said, "I Paul, the prisoner of Jesus Christ."

It doesn't take a Bible scholar to know that Jesus Christ did not put Paul in prison. He was put there by people for preaching about Jesus.

Yet, Paul had a strong belief that when he was saved that he became a son of God. So, if he was a son of God, he could honestly declare, "I am a prisoner of Jesus Christ."

It did not matter that he was in jail. "What" he was in couldn't take away "who" he was the son of.

The same goes for you today. No matter what situation you are in, you are a child of God.

Gravity says, "What goes up must come down."

The grave says, "What goes down must come up."

Yes, as a Christian I believe in the resurrection!

1 Thessalonians 4:16

For the Lord himself shall descend from heaven with a shout, with the voice of the archangel, and with the trump of God: and the dead in Christ shall rise first:

Nothing on the *exterior* should make you *inferior* if all is right in the *interior*.

In Philippians 3, Paul encouraged us to forget those things which are behind, and reach forth unto those things which are before.

In Psalm 23, David encouraged us to let the Lord be our Shepherd. He said, "The Lord is my Shepherd, I shall not want. He makes me lie down in green pastures; He leads me beside the still waters."

Sometimes in life, when you forget the things behind you and are reaching forth for the things before you, you need to take a moment and enjoy what the Lord has placed beside you.

The still waters beside you are where your soul is restored to recover from what is behind you and receive strength for what is before you.

When you are a dreamer, drama will follow you. Ask Joseph.

His brothers stirred up drama until they sold him. When he went to work for Potipher, the dreamer met the ultimate drama queen, who was the wife of his boss.

His family drama and the drama at his work tried to take away his dreams, but Joseph refused to be caught up in everyone else's negativity. He was born for a dream, not drama. Ultimately it paid off, and every dream he had dreamed came to pass.

Which is more powerful in your life, your dreams or your drama?

In Ezekiel 37, the Lord took Ezekiel to a valley of very dry bones.

In Ezekiel 47, the Lord took him to a very wet river.

As a Pastor, the Lord has to take me to both dry and wet places to relate to where everyone is in life.

Interestingly, in our Church, everyone is not in the same place. People have seasons in their life too. But unlike the weather, people can be sitting side by side in the same building and be going through a different season. While some are in a drought, others are experiencing a flood.

But even though we are not all at the same season at the same time, more than likely someone sitting beside you has already been through the season you are experiencing now.

Don't give up or give in; God will always let His Word reach you at the place where you presently reside.

Ecclesiastes 3:1
To every thing there is a season, and a time to every purpose under the heaven:

It doesn't matter how *baaaaaad* you've been. The Spotless Lamb specializes in rescuing the black sheep of the family.

Behold the Lamb of God that takes away the sin of the world.

Try Jesus. You will love him. To be God, He is so down to earth.

Thomas Edison had a *bright idea*. *Watt* is yours?

I admire people that work hard and provide for their families. It's not just a duty; it is a command.

However, as you go to work today, remember that life is not about your *income*; it's about your *outcome*.

How to have a good outcome is very easy. When Jesus called you, He merely said, "Come."

After you come to Him, He helps you become like Him. After you become like Him, you can overcome anything with Him.

Matthew 11:28
Come unto me, all ye that labour and are heavy laden, and I will you rest.

2 Corinthians 5:17
Therefore if any man be in Christ, he is a new creature: old things are passed away; behold, all things are become new.

1 John 2:13
I write unto you, fathers, because ye have known him that is from the beginning. I write unto you, young

men, because ye have overcome the wicked one. I write unto you, little children, because ye have known the Father.

The Lamb of God didn't just go out on a *limb* for you. He hung on a *tree*.

> Revelation 13:8
> ...the Lamb slain from the foundation of the world.

> Acts 5:30
> The God of our fathers raised up Jesus, whom ye slew and hung on a tree.

Don't worry about all of the ugly stuff that you go through. Soon it will turn and be beautiful.

> Ecc. 3:11
> He has made everything beautiful in His time.

Abraham was called the Father of the Faithful.

God promised him that his seed would be as the sand of the seas and the stars in the Heavens. God told him to count the stars. That was awesome on clear nights, but how is a man supposed to do that when it's cloudy?

Number 1, on those clear nights, get so familiar with the stars that you know where they are, even when they are covered with clouds.

Number 2, when the clouds won't let you count, you can still count on the One who made the stars and told you to count them!

God is counting on you to count whatever He has called you to do. Whether it's clear or cloudy, you can count on Him to be there with you!

The posture of prayer on your knees will result in the power of prayer in your walk.

The impossible in your crisis is possible because of the cross.

As the *apple* of God's eye, you must have *core* values.

Psalm 17:8
Keep me as the apple of your eye; hide me in the shadow of your wings.

John 6:9
There is a lad here, which hath five barley loaves, and
two small fishes: but what are they among so many?

The little guy with five loaves and two fish had no idea that
his lunch would launch him into greatness.

All God wants is for you to know that if you give him your
little bit, He can do a whole lot.

Chapter 8
Following and Leading

S ome people would rather see you fall than watch you fly. Fly anyway.

Getting on our knees is the only thing that can change what is in our news.

2 Chronicles 7:14
If my people, which are called by my name, shall humble themselves, and pray, and seek my face, and turn from their wicked ways; then will I hear from heaven, and will forgive their sin, and will heal their land.

People in your corner is good; Jesus on your cross is better.

The Bible is very clear that satan is as a roaring lion seeking whom he may devour. We should always be on guard for his treacherous traps.

However, the Bible is also very clear that we are to abstain from the very appearance of evil. Many of our "spiritual" attacks aren't spiritual at all. In fact, they are quite the opposite.

The devil did not attack Samson; Samson was attracted to Delilah. We all know the sadness of this fatal attraction. He was merely attracted to her then attacked by her.

Today, be on guard against both the spiritual and natural attacks. It may be the devil, but it may be Delilah. With the Spirit living in you, you have the power to withstand both!

If God led you to it,
He will lead you through it.

One of the most interesting verses in the Bible was at the beginning of Jesus's ministry.

Matthew 4:1
Then was Jesus led up of the Spirit into the wilderness to be tempted of the devil.

Yes, it says that the Spirit led Jesus into the wilderness.

We don't think that the Spirit will lead us to those kinds of places, especially to be tempted by the devil.

But, rest assured, if God brought you to it, He will bring you through it!

Birds of a feather flock together. Then there's you...

Stop thinking that you don't fit in, and start thanking God that you do stand out!

When God made man, He intended to meet him every morning in the MIST.

> Genesis 2:6-7
> But there went up a MIST from the earth, and watered the whole face of the ground. And the LORD God formed man of the dust of the ground, and breathed into his nostrils the breath of life; and man became a living soul.

Then, in the New Testament, Jesus talked about meeting with others and promised that He would be there in the MIDST.

> Matthew 18:20
> For where two or three are gathered together in my name, there am I in the MIDST of them.

My take away from these two verses:

I need my alone time in the morning MIST with my Maker. Then, I need time with His other children during the day, and He promised to show up in the MIDST.

Don't MISS the MIST or the MIDST!

Just because you suffered a loss doesn't make you a loser. Sometimes, loss is God's way of being your life preserver.

> Luke 17:33
> Whosoever shall seek to save his life shall lose it; and whosoever shall lose his life shall preserve it.

Just any old song won't open prison doors. It takes a song of praise. If the songs in our churches are not opening doors and shutting down the devil, we might need to change our tune.

> Acts 16:25
> And at midnight Paul and Silas prayed and sang praises unto God: and the prisoners heard them. 26 And suddenly there was a great earthquake, so that the foundations of the prison were shaken: and immediately all the doors were opened.

I have no reason to believe that there is a pot of gold at the end of a rainbow, but I have every reason to believe that there is a street of gold under the rainbow.

Rev. 4:3
And he that sat was to look upon like a jasper and a sardine stone: and there was a rainbow round about the throne, in sight like unto an emerald.

Rev. 21:21
And the twelve gates were twelve pearls; every several gate was of one pearl: and the street of the city was pure gold, as it were transparent glass.

The prodigal son was far from home, but he wasn't far from hope. The moment he came to himself and said, "I will arise and go to my Father," hope came into his heart, and he headed home.

I don't know how far you are away from home today, but hope is just one heartbeat away. I hope you will head home to God's will for your life!

Hebrews 12:1
Wherefore seeing we also are compassed about with so great a cloud of witnesses, let us lay aside every weight, and the sin which doth so easily beset us, and let us run with patience the race that is set before us...

Allow patience to be your running partner...
Let us run *with* patience.

You can't live life thinking-*what if I fail.* You have to live it thinking-*when I succeed.*

God's will... will give you power that your *willpower* can't match.

When you know that God has a *plan* for your life, you don't have to worry about the devil's *plot* for your life.

One appointment with the *Great Physician* can heal the hurts that you have *nursed* for years.

Matthew 9:12
But when Jesus heard that, he said unto them, they that
be whole need not a physician, but they that are sick.

Comeback-that thing that happened after your setback.

Proverbs 24:16
For a just man falls seven times, and rises up again.

As strange as it may sound, someone talking about your past could be a compliment. It means they have no new material from your present.

Imitate Christ; *intimidate* the devil.

1 Thessalonians 1:6
You became imitators of us and of the Lord, for you welcomed the message in the midst of severe suffering with the joy given by the Holy Spirit.

Hey devil!
My Father's *arm* is larger than your *army*!

Isaiah 52:10
The Lord has made bare his holy arm in the eyes of all the nations; and all the ends of the earth shall see the salvation of our God.

Hebrews 11:34

Quenched the violence of fire, escaped the edge of the sword, out of weakness were made strong, waxed valiant in fight, turned to flight the armies of the aliens.

When you *cast* your cares on Jesus, it takes away the urge to *throw* in the towel.

Whether it's exercise or executing a new life plan, it takes more than someone to inspire you.

You have to perspire to help it happen.

The end result makes the sweat sweet.

When you scream, "I CAN'T DO THIS ANYMORE," it's not a defeat. It's an acceptance. The moment you decide you can't do it on your own is the moment that Jesus knows He is free to help you.

1 Corinthians 10:13
There hath no temptation taken you but such as is common to man: but God is faithful, who will not suffer you to be tempted above that ye are able; but will with the temptation also make a way to escape,

that ye may be able to bear it.

If you don't know where you are spiritually and you feel lost, dial Psalm 91:1.

Psalms 91:1
He that dwells in the secret place of the most High shall abide under the shadow of the Almighty.

It's important to let what brings you to tears bring you to your knees.

What brings you to your knees is designed to bring you closer to God.

What brings you closer to God will turn your tears of sorrow into tears of joy!

Psalm 126:5
They that sow in tears shall reap in joy.

The things that happen *to me* also happen to be the things that will mold me into what I am meant *to be*.

Philippians 1:12,19

But I would ye should understand, brethren, that the things which happened unto me have fallen out rather unto the furtherance of the gospel.

For I know that this shall turn to my salvation through your prayer, and the supply of the Spirit of Jesus Christ.

Your life will never be a *Fairy Tale*, but that's okay. People will benefit much more when they read your *True Story*.

The things that satan sent to *shake* me, God used to *shape* me.

2 Thessalonians 2:2

That ye be not soon shaken in mind, or be troubled, neither by spirit, nor by word, nor by letter as from us, as that the day of Christ is at hand.

1 Corinthians 10:13

There hath no temptation taken you but such as is common to man: but God is faithful, who will not suffer you to be tempted above that ye are able; but will with the temptation also make a way to escape, that ye may be able to bear it.

Peace is not the *absence* of conflict; it is the *presence* of the Comforter.

> John 14:16, 27
> And I will pray the Father, and he shall give you another Comforter, that he may abide with you forever. Peace I leave with you, my peace I give unto you: not as the world giveth, give I unto you. Let not your heart be troubled, neither let it be afraid.

People make a mountain out of a molehill, and then pray they that God will move the mountain.

I certainly believe that the Bible is accurate when it says that we can speak to mountains and they will move.

When Jesus said that, He was referring to insurmountable situations that are entirely out of our control. I have seen many mountains move in my Christian walk.

However, there have been a few mountains that were still there after I prayed.

After enquiring of the Lord as to why they didn't move, He let me know that not all mountains are created equal. In fact, there are mountains that He created, and there are mountains that I created. The ones that I created were mostly mountains that I made out of molehills.

As humans, we have the propensity to take small issues and make them large matters. Things that we should walk around or simply walk over become things that we have to climb up.

So, sometimes our mountains need us to get on our knees so we begin to pray that God will move them. But sometimes, we need to get a shovel or maybe a bulldozer and push down the thing that we made so big.

Some mountains that need to be moved weren't created by God at the beginning of time. They were created by us at the beginning of a situation that we don't know how to handle.

Matthew 21:21
Jesus replied, Truly I tell you, if you have faith and do not doubt, not only can you do what was done to the fig tree, but also you can say to this mountain, 'Go, throw yourself into the sea,' and it will be done.

The only way that you can *empower* people is to *embody* Christ.

1 Corinthians 2:4
And my speech and my preaching was not with enticing words of man's wisdom, but in demonstration of the Spirit and of power.

He who is approved by God should not spend time trying to prove himself to people.

2 Timothy 2:15
Study to show thyself approved unto God, a workman that needs not to be ashamed, rightly dividing the

word of truth.

Acts 25:7
And when he was come, the Jews which came down
from Jerusalem stood round about, and laid many and
grievous complaints against Paul, which they could
not prove.

When *opportunity* knocks, the *opposition* will barge in.

1 Timothy 6:20
O Timothy, keep that which is committed to thy trust,
avoiding profane and vain babblings, and oppositions
of science falsely so called:

A true leader does not just want people's *output*; they
respect people's *input*.

People who live to make everybody happy live a very sad life.

Don't focus on the one *Judas* that *betrayed* you; focus on
the other *eleven* that *believed* you.

Acts 1:13
And when they were come in, they went up into an upper room, where abode both Peter, and James, and John, and Andrew, Philip, and Thomas, Bartholomew, and Matthew, James the son of Alphaeus, and Simon Zelotes, and Judas the brother of James.

Even when you speak the truth in love, someone will brand it as hate speech.
Speak it anyway.
Love anyway.

As a 59-year-old man, I have been given many opportunities. However, as much as I try to be content, I daily push myself to do everything I feel God has called me to do. There are so many things that I want to accomplish that, so far in my life, I've not yet attained.

But, if you were to ask me what's the one thing that I would like to do that seems unattainable, I would have to say that I would like to write a new vocabulary.

Yes, I know that sounds far-fetched, but I'm troubled by some good words that we use to describe normal things, and then we use those same words to describe God.

We say that was a great steak, and then we say what a great God we serve. We say that was a good burger, and then we talk about a good God. Incredible house, incredible God; Awesome movie, awesome God; Fabulous purse, fabulous God; Super car, super God; WOW factor, and WOW, what a God! On and on and on I could go.

Sadly, I can't coin a phrase or write a poem of praise to change our vocabulary. But one thing I can do is tell you this for sure: God is the awe in awesome. He put the fab in fabulous. He's the credible part of incredible, and the God in good. And any way that you spell it, He is WOW spelled frontward and backward!

You should never hear a preacher say, "Don't try this at home." A church is where your faith is *refined*, and home is where your faith is *defined*.

As a Pastor, I always smile when people stop looking at Christianity as *rules* with *regulations* and understand it is a *relationship* with *revelations*.

Live your life so that what *transpires inspires* someone else. For when you *expire*, that's all you'll have.

Your reputation is not built on what you *meant* to do. It's built on doing what you were *sent* to do.

Everyone in the Bible that interpreted someone else's dreams was a dreamer. Don't ever expect people to believe in your dreams if they have none of their own.

The miracle of the loaves and fish is one of the most famous stories in the Bible. Thousands of people were gathered to hear Jesus teach, but only one person brought lunch.

Most people have heard this story of the little lad's lunch. However, I thought about something yesterday that I've never considered. We know that Jesus multiplied the loaves and fish and fed 5,000 men plus the women and children. But what I wonder is whether or not he altered the taste?

Probably not. The taste of the food and the way it was prepared were most likely the same as the food in the lad's lunchbox. I imagine the taste buds in those thousands of mouths tasted the exact taste that the little boy had prepared.

But it's safe to say that he left a good taste in the mouths of everyone that enjoyed his multiplied cuisine.

Today, I desire to leave a good taste in the mouths of all the people that I meet. I certainly need God to multiply my efforts, but I will prepare my little bit, just in case what I do today will impact the taste buds of a world in which other Christians have left a bad taste.

Every Sunday, I preach to the *conscious*, the *subconscious*, the *unconscious*, and those that seem to have *no conscience*.

I would much rather deal with someone who is *wrong* and *repentant* than someone who is *right* but *rude*.

True Biblical preaching is exemplified by putting people in water because of the Word, without watering down the Word.

Through the years, I've met a lot of people that wanted a powerful preacher to keep them on the edge of their seats, the same seats they rarely came to church and sat on it.

Our *compassion* for reaching the *lost* needs to be greater than our *passion* for preaching to the *saved*.

The greatest insult a Pastor can get occurs when, at the end of his sermon, every head is already bowed and every eye is already closed.

Acts 20:9
And there sat in a window a certain young man named Eutychus, being fallen into a deep sleep: and as Paul was long preaching, he sunk down with sleep, and

fell down from the third loft, and was taken up dead.

This is a sad verse that ends up funny. Paul was preaching too long, and Eutychus went into a deep sleep. What's unfortunate for Paul is that he never even got to say the Pastor's favorite quote, "Every head bowed, and every eye closed."

This young man bowed his head and closed his eyes way before Paul was through.

If you read the rest of the story, Paul prayed for Eutychus and raised him from the dead. So, I guess my point to all of us preachers is that before you say, "Every head bowed, and every eye closed," make sure that the people have not already done that.

At least shout, "HALLELUJAH," real loud and wake them up, then you can have them to bow their heads and close their eyes again.

People, in general, perform a lot better when they are *cheered on* than when they are *chewed out*.

Time is our greatest commodity.

Anything that is worth having takes a lot of time. However, time has to be managed. Not everything or everyone you spend your time on is always worth the effort. Not all things nor all people will change, no matter how much you "fixate" your energy toward that goal.

Sometimes, time has to be evaluated, and you have to move on to things that merit the time it takes to make it a wise investment.

Spend your time on things or people that have the desire to be changed into the image of God.

If indeed time is money, you have to "budget" who to spend time on. Some people are a *deposit* of your time, while others are simply making a *withdrawal*.

No one should ever receive *cash* for preaching the gospel that hasn't had a real *change*. Neither should they accept *cash*, if they do not give God *credit*.

As a Pastor, I love to preach the *profound* truth to old Christians, but the most joy I have is preaching the *newfound* truth to new converts!

If you follow me on social media, or if I'm your Pastor, you know that I love words. But truthfully, I love the Word of God more than anything else. Like most "middle-age" men, I have a desire to see the Word of God go from generation to generation. I want to provide leadership for every age bracket.

But it seems nowadays that Preachers are succumbing to the pressure of being hip. Yes, I finally broke down and wore jeans to Wednesday services, but you will still see me wearing a suit and tie on Sunday.

I've decided that I am who I am, and I'm okay with the fact that I'm not what some in this generation want preachers to be.

So, with the way that I look at words, this is my brand of leadership: The people that I lead will say, "My Pastor provides *leaderSHIP*." But they will probably never say, "My *leader's HIP*."

Pastors are not the police. If we "catch" you sinning, we will not give you a ticket. All we can do is issue a warning.

Most of my sermons are meant to *warm* your heart. However, there are times that I have to preach something that will *warn* your heart.

Every person that works for God is required to work with people. And Jesus taught that the way you treat the people you work with is a direct correlation of your commitment to the God you work for.

Moses was a man of many mountains. It was on a mountain where God showed him many wonders. From this mountain, we have the information about Creation as well as the Ten Commandments. But it was also at a mountain where Moses messed up. God told him to speak to it, and because of anger, he instead hit it with his anointed rod.

Be careful how you respond *on* a mountain and at a mountain. On the mountain, God revealed His past, and at a mountain, God revealed Moses' future.

Preaching is not for me to *impress* you with my abilities; it is for me to *impact* you to go and find yours.

Change is a part of life. Most of the people in the civilized world change clothes on a daily basis. We change the sheets on our bed and the filter in our furnace. We change the oil in our car and the thermostat on our air unit. We change the radio station when we don't like the song and the TV station when we don't like the program. We change careers and change jobs. On and on I could go about things that we change on a daily basis.

As a Pastor, I see the constant need for change, and I am certainly not afraid to change an idea or a concept or even a service time. But, Churches change because the people that attend the Churches change. Our schedules change, our careers change, our family dynamics change, our styles change, and our way of doing so many things change.

Change is so common that if the Church we attend doesn't change to the way that some think they should change, then it's easy for people to change Churches.

I will be the first to admit that sometimes God does call people to change Churches. We have been both the recipient of some great people changing to come to our Church, as well as the Church that some great people changed from. All of that is part of the process of being the Pastor of a local Church.

During the 23 years that I have been blessed to Pastor the beautiful people at Word of Life, I have not one time ever withheld a blessing from someone who told me that God had told them to change Churches. My thought is – who am I to say no to you if God spoke to you.

However, I'm keenly aware that it's not always God that tells people to change Churches. Sometimes when God says change, it's meant for the individual or family to change themselves.

It's so much easier to change Churches than it is to change yourself.

The Bible says that in the multitude of counsel there is safety. I firmly believe in Godly counsel and advice. However, no one can give you advice on your dreams. They are your dreams. Only God can interpret them.

God does not comply when the preacher says, "Every head bowed, and every eye closed." When my eyes are closed, His are open, seeing what I need. I'm so glad that He is an all-seeing God!

> 2 Chronicles 16:9
> For the EYES OF THE LORD run to and fro throughout the whole earth, to shew himself strong in the behalf of them whose heart is perfect toward him.

Depending on who you ask about me, the answer could be different. More than once, as a leader, conservatives have called me liberal, and liberals have called me conservative. I am not swayed by what they call me because God calls me His child.

In my ministry, I've witnessed more people healed from *mental illness* than I have seen delivered from *judgmental illness*.

> Matthew 7:1-2
> Judge not, that ye be not judged. For with what judgment ye judge, ye shall be judged: and with what measure ye mete, it shall be measured to you again.

Some people want to dilute the gospel by watering it down and taking away its potency. Others want to pollute the gospel with man-made additives to make it palatable to their man-made doctrine.

The Word of God needs to be what God said, not what I said He said. Paul told Timothy to preach the Word!

When we preach God's Word, God's way, it's no problem knowing God's will!

Rev. 22:18-19

For I testify unto every man that hears the words of the prophecy of this book, If any man shall ADD UNTO these things, God shall add unto him the plagues that are written in this book:

And if any man shall TAKE AWAY from the words of the book of this prophecy, God shall take away his part out of the book of life, and out of the holy city, and from the things which are written in this book.

Jesus seemed to enjoy *sitting with sinners* more than He enjoyed *running with the religious*.

Jesus deemed it more necessary to sit with a *kid* on His *lap* than as a *King* on His *throne*.

When preaching impresses you, you say *amen*, and the Preacher preaches better.

When preaching empowers you, the Preacher says *amen*, and you live better.

Preaching wasn't invented by God to *impress* people. It was given to *empower* them.

One of the joys of being a true Bible Pastor is that my answers don't have to be *scripted*. They have to be *Scriptures*.

If we will say what God said, it doesn't matter who we offend because our only obligation is to quote God. It's never because I said so but because God said so. I concur with what Paul told Timothy, "Preach the Word!"

> 2 Timothy 4:2
> Preach the word; be instant in season, out of season; reprove, rebuke, exhort with all longsuffering and doctrine.

A *manual* is defined as a handbook for giving instructions... how to do something using human effort, skill, power, or energy.

Emmanuel is defined as God with us. His handbook is a Holy Book. It is also used for instructions. However, it teaches you how to live, but not in your human effort, skill, power, and energy. It instructs us on how to go from *God with us* to *God in us*.

Pastors are a little like football coaches. We can instruct you to do the "plays" that we've seen work hundreds of times.

Pastors are also like baseball managers. We have to put people in the right positions to manage the "game."

Pastors are also like golf caddies. We have the vision for the "shot" that you should take.

However, the difference in a Pastor and all of these things mentioned above is that you as a Christian have a choice in whether or not you will accept our recommendation. We do not pay you to show up, but we pray that you will.

> Ephesians 4:11-12
> And he gave some, apostles; and some, prophets; and some, evangelists; and some, pastors and teachers; for the perfecting of the saints, for the work of the ministry, for the edifying of the body of Christ:

I LOVE MY JOB!

Someone brought me some authentic, pure olive oil from Greece. Interestingly, they put it in a Crown Royal bottle. My mind won't stop:

- God specializes in taking old containers and putting new things in it.
- Whatever you have used your life for in the past has passed. Now, God will take you, and use you, and anoint you.

- We have this treasure in earthen vessels.
- You anoint my head with oil.
- If there is any sick among you, let them call for the elders of the church and let them pray over him anointing him with oil in the name of the Lord. The prayer of faith shall save the sick, and if he has committed sin it shall be forgiven.
- Man looks on the outward appearance, but God looks on the heart.
- It's what's inside that counts.

God will take you from CROWN ROYAL to a ROYAL CROWN!

> 2 Timothy 4:8
> Henceforth there is laid up for me a crown of righteousness, which the Lord, the righteous judge, shall give me at that day: and not to me only, but unto all them also that love his appearing.

Jesus came to change His Ministers from *Law enforcers* to *grace endorsers*.

As a preacher, I do not preach for a *response*. I preach because of *responsibility*.

1 Corinthians 9:16
For though I preach the gospel, I have nothing to glory of: for necessity is laid upon me; yea, woe is unto me, if I preach not the gospel!

Even if people say, "It's a *good sermon,*" if it's not a *God sermon,* it's not valid.

2 Timothy 4:2
Preach the word; be instant in season, out of season; reprove, rebuke, exhort with all longsuffering and doctrine.

A cardinal rule for Ministers:
If someone compliments you, don't let it go to your head. If someone gives you criticism, don't let it go to your heart.

I don't know which is more annoying: those that answer every question or those that question every answer.

A wounded world needs a healing Word.

Isaiah 53:5
But he was wounded for our transgressions, he
was bruised for our iniquities: the chastisement of
our peace was upon him; and with his stripes we
are healed.

Psalm 147:3
He healeth the broken in heart, and bindeth up
their wounds.

A faithful servant is one who sets up the stage for someone
else to sit on.

Galatians 5:13
For, brethren, ye have been called unto liberty; only
use not liberty for an occasion to the flesh, but by love
serve one another.

Pastor–One who prays for *revival* on Sunday and *arrival*
on Wednesday.

Esther was a *maid* by trade, but she was *made* to be a Queen.

When Elisha picked up the fallen mantle of Elijah, he did not dismantle it. Too many younger ministers are *dismantling* the *mantle* that was meant to bring miracles. Using the mantle like it was intended will double the miracles.

The key to *leading* by example is to follow by example.

It's impossible to be a good leader if you are not a good follower.

True Bible preaching is exemplified by putting people in water because of the Word without watering down the Word.

When Peter started drowning, Jesus gave him a hand and saved him, then gave him a sermon.

Drowning people need someone to save them and bring them to the boat, then preach the sermon.

Too often we see people drowning in sin or stupidity, and we preach them a sermon while they are going under. But if you will save the sermon and help the person to safety, they will quickly realize that you saved them. Then, you can give them the sermon, and they will know what to do next time.

So much of social media is screaming at people that we perceive to be doing stupid stuff. If Jesus is indeed our life, why don't we try to be a "life jacket" and help them out, instead of talking about how stupid they are as they drown?

Often people feel that they have to choose sides. It seems that when we pick a side, the other side gets upset. But to get more personal, we always want everyone to choose our side of whatever battle the day brings. We even quote the verse from Psalm 118:6, "The Lord is on my side."

But could it be that the Lord is on the side of both parties? I believe the Bible clearly states that at times He most certainly is. In fact, His crucifixion is the best example.

On either side of Jesus, a thief was crucified with Him. One of the thieves asked Jesus to remember him when Jesus came into His Kingdom. The other thief rebuked his fellow thief and said, "He is in the same shape as we are."

Hence, one side was right, and one side was wrong, but Jesus was on the side of each of them.

Sometimes you don't choose sides; sides choose you.

Real leaders have a *same-day* mentality in a *someday* world.

> Hebrews 3:13
> But encourage one another daily, as long as it is called "Today," so that none of you may be hardened by sin's deceitfulness.

Usually, people that are always putting people in their place are people that need to be put in their place.

Having a command of the Scriptures is powerful. Obeying the commands is more powerful.

We do not need *handcrafted* words of man. We need the *engrafted* Word of God.

James 1:21
Wherefore lay apart all filthiness and superfluity of naughtiness, and receive with meekness the engrafted word, which is able to save your souls.

I can *pray* for your blessing without *prying* into your business.

As a Pastor, sometimes I'm granted a little "inside" information into the maladies within the lives of people needing a miracle. However, some people are very private and are not comfortable sharing the shame that they are facing.

While you can tell me everything in confidence, you don't have to tell me anything to get me to pray for you. The bottom line is that God knows all about everything you are facing. I'm good with praying for your blessing without prying into your business.

If you need to talk, we will talk; but either way, I'll talk to God about your need. I'm praying for you today!

Popular people will eventually lose their popularity, but honorable people will never lose their honor.

I am more concerned about those that don't wake before they die than those that die before they wake.

> Romans 13:11
> And that, knowing the time, that now it is high time to awake out of sleep: for now is our salvation nearer than when we believed.

While Christianity is eagerly endorsing whoever might be the currently coolest Christian, the world is frantically trying to find the kindest.

I will never spend time trying to be the coolest, but I will daily strive to be the kindest.

#UNKINDISUNCOOL

> Romans 12:10
> Be kindly affectioned one to another with brotherly love; in honour preferring one another;

Leadership is the ability to better others without making them feel like you are better than them.

Chapter 9
Words of Wisdom

True wisdom is not letting everything that goes through your mind come out of your mouth.

Ephesians 4:29
Let no corrupt communication proceed out of your mouth, but that which is good to the use of edifying, that it may minister grace unto the hearers.

Psalm 19:14
Let the words of my mouth, and the meditation of my heart, be acceptable in thy sight, O Lord, my strength, and my redeemer.

Tired of traffic jams?
Take the high road.
Traffic is light on the high road, and there is no road rage.

Part of daily discipline is the ability to *train* your mind to stay on track.

Philippians 4:8-9
Finally, brothers, whatsoever things are true, whatsoever things are honest, whatsoever things are just, whatsoever things are pure, whatsoever things are lovely, whatsoever things are of good report; if there be any virtue, and if there be any praise, think on these things. Those things, which ye have both learned, and received, and heard, and seen in me, do: and the God of peace shall be with you.

As you size up your *situation*, don't forget the size of your *Savior*.

1 Samuel 17:45-50
Then said David to the Philistine, Thou comest to me with a sword, and with a spear, and with a shield: but I come to thee in the name of the Lord of hosts, the God of the armies of Israel, whom thou hast defied. This day will the Lord deliver thee into mine hand; and I will smite thee, and take thine head from thee; and I will give the carcasses of the host of the Philistines this day unto the fowls of the air, and to the wild beasts of the earth; that all the earth may know that there is a God in Israel. And all this assembly shall

know that the Lord saves not with sword and spear: for the battle is the Lord's, and he will give you into our hands.

And it came to pass, when the Philistine arose, and came and drew nigh to meet David that David hasted, and ran toward the army to meet the Philistine. And David put his hand in his bag, and took thence a stone, and slang it, and smote the Philistine in his forehead that the stone sunk into his forehead; and he fell upon his face to the earth. So David prevailed over the Philistine with a sling and with a stone, and smote the Philistine, and slew him; but there was no sword in the hand of David.

To have *peace* of mind, you have to stop giving others a *piece* of your mind.

Proverbs 29:11
A fool vents all his feelings, but a wise man holds them back.

Romans 14:19
Let us therefore follow after the things which make for peace, and things wherewith one may edify another.

Joseph was a dreamer. He knew that what God revealed to him in dreams was his future. However, his brothers and others dismissed him as arrogant. His story in Genesis is worth the read. It took 13 years of "nightmares" before he saw his dream fulfilled.

Even though this story is so familiar, I noticed something this morning that I think is noteworthy.

Whether it was his brothers, Potiphar's wife, or the people in prison, Joseph never fought with them. But he did keep fighting for his dream.

So remember that if people didn't give you the dream, there's no need to fight with them when they don't believe what God has given you.

Keep dreaming. Soon you will see the fulfillment of what God gave you.

True wisdom is learning how to *fight for* your dream without *fighting with* people who don't believe it.

Never put your money in a vending machine that *doesn't* work.

Never give your money to a person that *won't* work.

2 Thessalonians 3:10
For even when we were with you, this we commanded you, that if any would not work, neither should he eat.

When you figure God in, you never have to figure life out.

Isaiah 30:21
And thine ears shall hear a word behind thee, saying,
This is the way, walk ye in it, when ye turn to the right
hand, and when ye turn to the left.

As Christians, we have to learn how to fight *for* people
without fighting *with* them.

Ephesians 6:12
For we wrestle not against flesh and blood, but against
principalities, against powers, against the rulers of the
darkness of this world, against spiritual wickedness
in high places.

Don't allow the negative things that happened *to* you to
also happen *in* you.

Ephesians 4:31
Let all bitterness, and wrath, and anger, and clamor,
and evil speaking, be put away from you, with
all malice:

Be careful with your words.

235

You may be strong enough to say something and forget it, but someone who hears you may remember what you said for a lifetime.

> Colossians 4:6
> Let your conversation be always full of grace, seasoned with salt.

I can't help but wonder how many people are currently sleeping in a cemetery who never awoke to the revelation of who they are in Christ.

We teach our kids to pray if they should *die before they wake*, but we need to teach them the importance of making sure to *wake before they die*.

> Romans 13:11
> And that, knowing the time, that now it is high time to awake out of sleep: for now is our salvation nearer than when we believed.

I have little tolerance for healthy people that *won't* work, and I have the same disdain for people that keep repeating the same ways that *don't* work.

Philosophies that don't work are just as detrimental as people that won't work.

Colossians 2:8

Beware lest any man spoil you through philosophy and vain deceit, after the tradition of men, after the rudiments of the world, and not after Christ.

Don't let the people that break your heart also break your spirit. It's easier to rebound from a broken heart than from a broken spirit.

Proverbs 18:14

The spirit of a man will sustain his infirmity; but a wounded spirit who can bear?

Proverbs 18:19

A brother offended is harder to be won than a strong city: and their contentions are like the bars of a castle.

Thinking out loud can sometimes be interpreted as speaking without thinking.

Before *push* comes to shove, make sure the door doesn't say *pull*.

Christian wisdom is learning how to *embrace* people without *endorsing* their behavior.

John 8:11
She said, No man, Lord. And Jesus said unto her, Neither do I condemn thee: go, and sin no more.

For every *what if*, there is a *why not*. *Why not* stop worrying about *what if?*

The best remedy when your back is against the wall is to put your knees against the floor. Place head in hands and begin to pray.

Daniel 6:6-10
Then these presidents and princes assembled together to the king, and said thus unto him, King Darius, live for ever. All the presidents of the kingdom, the governors, and the princes, the counsellors, and the captains, have consulted together to establish a royal statute, and to make a firm decree, that whosoever shall ask a petition of any God or man for thirty days, save of thee, O king, he shall be cast into the den of lions. Now, O king, establish the decree, and sign the writing, that it be not changed, according to the

law of the Medes and Persians, which altereth not. Wherefore king Darius signed the writing and the decree. Now when Daniel knew that the writing was signed, he went into his house; and his windows being open in his chamber toward Jerusalem, he kneeled upon his knees three times a day, and prayed, and gave thanks before his God, as he did aforetime.

Backup cameras in automobiles are cool inventions, but I've noticed that they only work in reverse. You can only see what's behind you when you are going backward. These handy devices aren't meant to be used for long periods of times, but just long enough to keep you from doing damage that will prevent you from going forward. Your backup camera and reverse gear were never meant to be used more than a few seconds.

There are many times in life that you need to put your life in reverse. Reverse helps you turn around and move forward. You should never mind "backing out" of a situation that keeps you from moving ahead. Then, after you get back on the road, you can join with Paul in Philippians 3:13 and say, "But this one thing I do, forgetting those things which are behind, and reaching forth unto those things which are before."

Don't spend more on your *burial insurance* than your *resurrection assurance*.

You have no power to stop intermittent malfunctions in your life. However, you do have the ability to prevent the *malfunction* from becoming a *dysfunction*.

I choose to spend my time *defending* what I believe without being *offended* by those who don't agree with me.

James 3:2
For in many things we offend all. If any man offend not in word, the same is a perfect man, and able also to bridle the whole body.

Minding your manners is more than *chewing* with your mouth *closed*.
It's *choosing* what comes out when your mouth is *open*.

Colossians 4:6
Let your speech be alway with grace, seasoned with salt, that ye may know how ye ought to answer every man.

Disagreeing with people is okay. It's not okay to *disrespect* them.

James 2:9
But if ye have respect to persons, ye commit sin, and are convinced of the law as transgressors.

Don't get caught up in the current of current events.

Mark 13:19-22
For in those days shall be affliction, such as was not from the beginning of the creation which God created unto this time, neither shall be. And except that the Lord had shortened those days, no flesh should be saved: but for the elect's sake, whom he hath chosen, he hath shortened the days. And then if any man shall say to you, Lo, here is Christ; or, lo, he is there; believe him not: For false Christs and false prophets shall rise, and shall show signs and wonders, to seduce, if it were possible, even the elect.

You will always *struggle* as long as you *smuggle* past hurts into your present situations.

Philippians 3:13
Brethren, I count not myself to have apprehended: but this one thing I do, forgetting those things which are behind, and reaching forth unto those things which are before.

Remember, what you say will become what you said.
People will always base what you say now on what you said then.

Live your life so that when you are up in years you can speak of *back in the day* with fondness.

Psalm 90:9
For all our days are passed away in thy wrath: we spend our years as a tale that is told.

Your *soul* motivation should be your *sole* motivation.

1 Peter 4:19
Wherefore let them that suffer according to the will of God commit the keeping of their souls to him in well

doing, as unto a faithful Creator.

Philippians 3:13
Brethren, I count not myself to have apprehended: but this one thing I do, forgetting those things which are behind, and reaching forth unto those things which are before,

Who is right is not always important. What is right always is.

Job 6:25
How forcible are right words! but what does your arguing reprove?

You are a *limited* edition, so stop trying to be a *rendition* of someone else!

I would much rather have the *unmerited favor* of God than the *unfavorable merits* of man.

Stop seeking approval from people that are looking for approval from people who give people approval ratings.

I'm not sure that I would want to know what my approval rating is… since the same people that approved of Jesus one day disapproved the next.

Our focus should always be to be God approved. If I am approved of God, I don't have to prove anything to you.

Once in a lifetime is not always an opportunity.

Matthew 16:26
For what is a man profited, if he shall gain the whole world, and lose his own soul? or what shall a man give in exchange for his soul?

Anything good takes time. Anything bad steals it.

There is no progress without process.

Greater is He that is in you than what others are putting on you.

I'm not opposed to the *newest trends* if they pass the test of possessing the *oldest truths*.

Please give me the honor of *nudging* you to go forward without you feeling like I'm *judging* where you are.

God's will for your life is not crumbled up in a cookie; it was crucified on a cross.

God's will is always revealed in His Word.

You will never find your answer in a fortune cookie, but you will always be fortunate because of the Cross.

In religion as well as relationships, after you have talked heart to heart and still don't see eye to eye, you can still walk hand in hand.

Don't jump... to conclusions.

Ecclesiastes 12:13
Let us hear the conclusion of the whole matter: Fear God, and keep his commandments: for this is the

whole duty of man.

Don't fixate on something you can't fix.

A symptom of dying is never learning how to live.

Unless you are filming a documentary where you are *portraying* Jesus, you need to stop playing Jesus in real life.

Remove the focus of what people do to you, and change it to what you do with what they did.

There are negative people interwoven into the fabric of all of our lives. However, when writing the book of your life, you should not give those negative naysayers more than a paragraph.

Your life story is about you, not them. If you give them more than a paragraph, that chapter becomes more about what they did to you than what you did to overcome whatever they did.

The only problem with running from yourself is you are always there when you get there.

God is the only person that you can run *from* and run *to* at the same time.

When words are used as weapons, someone always gets hurt. When words are used with wisdom, someone always gets helped.

> Colossians 4:6
> Let your conversation be always full of grace, seasoned with salt, so that you may know how to answer everyone.

The moment you realize that Jesus is The Way you will stop praying for Him to make a way.

Why is *nonsense* more common than *common sense*?

Does anyone other than me wish that common sense was one of the five senses?

Most people are born with five senses: Taste, smell, hearing, sight, and touch. Out of these five, four of them are located solely from the neck up.

The only one below the neck is the sense of touch or feel.

So, if 80 percent of our senses are above the neck and only 20 percent are below the neck, why do we spend so much time worrying about how we feel?

Something tells me that if we keep our head on straight and base life on what we know rather than what we feel, we will discover that God designed our lives to work out just fine.

Opportunity called. He said that his knuckles are sore from knocking. He wants you to answer. Every day that you ignore him is another missed opportunity. He wanted you to know that thousands of people were going to open the door tomorrow, but tomorrow never came. Today is another opportunity to open the door for opportunity.

It is better to be *vindicated* by God than *validated* by people.

A *better future* can only happen when you let go of a *bitter past*.

People that are *so in love* spend most of their time *sowing* love.

Don't allow a moment of weakness to give you a lifetime of weariness.

Views from the news are always skewed.
Views from the Bible are always reliable.

Jesus was not an American. He was not White, Black, Asian, or Hispanic. Neither was He a Pentecostal, Baptist, Methodist, or Catholic. He was and is the Son of God.

He will never fit into an American nor a religious mold. The sooner we try to be like Him and stop trying to make Him be like us, the sooner we will see His purpose fulfilled in the world for which He died.

In the beginning, if you will go the *altar route*, you will never have to be redirected to an *alternate route*.

Sometimes, you will break down on the journey of life. Situations will arise that will sideline you for a while. And yes, there are times that you need to pull over at the rest area and do just that-rest. But don't allow a temporary stall to impact the long haul. You started to finish, so don't let a little stall stop you!

Don't allow a *short stall* to impact the *long haul*.

As a Christian, it is possible to rub shoulders with worldly sinners without being pulled in to a secular system.

Be careful of the obvious.

In my sermon to our high school seniors last Sunday, I presented them with the "S" factor. Both sugar and salt obviously start with an s.

When I asked them to choose which was which, I couldn't hear the seniors for hearing the adults in the audience. People were shouting out, "The sugar is in the big container, and the salt is in the shaker."

People should know me by now. I put sugar in the salt shaker and salt in the sugar container. Just because salt and sugar look the same doesn't mean they are the same.

I can't preach the entire sermon here, but be careful of judging people by their looks. Sometimes, sweet comes in a shaker, and salty comes in the sugar bowl.

Be careful of the obvious.

Dealing with the pain of situations in life is one thing. Dealing with the people that have pleasure in your pain is another.

If you ever need false teeth, it is fine. But you should never need a false tongue.

Psalm 120:3
What shall be given unto thee? or what shall be done unto thee, thou false tongue.

You can be a real actor, but you can't act real.

Physical abuse is when people take their hands and beat you up. Verbal abuse is when people take their voice and beat you down.

All forms of abuse must be stopped! When words are used as weapons, someone is going to get wounded. Our hands weren't made to harm, and our voices weren't made for verbal violence.

Almost daily, we get the sad news of new violence. Bullying is bigger than ever. Seemingly, self-control is a fruit of the spirit that is rarely picked. Without restraint, everything in life is out of control.

God didn't make our hands to hurt people or to use a weapon to wound. Neither did He give us a voice to use for verbal violence. God doesn't want us to beat people up or to beat people down!

Lame is only an excuse if you really are.

It's okay to say *oops* now and then, but mistakes should never stop you. They should startle you to the point where the same error is not a repeated process.

Don't *wallow* in your pity.
Swallow your pride and try again.

Exasperation is being agitated about something negative that happened.

Expectation is anticipating something positive that will happen.

Today, I choose to live my life with expectation and not exasperation.

Sometimes gentle influences can be more detrimental than strong oppositions.

It's impossible to look up to God and look down on people.

Luke 9:48
And said unto them, Whosoever shall receive this child in my name receiveth me: and whosoever shall receive me receiveth him that sent me: for he that is least among you all, the same shall be great.

It's so much easier to *condemn* the faults of others than it is to *confess* your own.

Romans 8:34
Who is he that condemns? It is Christ that died, yea rather, that is risen again, who is even at the right hand of God, who also makes intercession for us.

James 5:16
Confess your faults one to another, and pray one for another, that ye may be healed. The effectual fervent prayer of a righteous man availeth much.

If your success is tied to the applause of people, you set yourself up for failure when no one is clapping.

Sometimes an educated guess becomes an uneducated mess.

In writing to the Church at Thessalonica, Paul addressed a unique subject for all to study. In 1 Thessalonians 4:11, he said for us to study to be quiet.

From the time we are born, we are encouraged to talk.

From the first words of *Dada* and *Mama*, people rejoice when children become fluent in their native language.

However, the older I get, even as talkative as I am, I am learning the importance of what James said in James 1:19: "My beloved brothers, let every man be swift to hear and slow to speak."

Sometimes, silence indeed is golden. There is a time when being fluent in silence could be better than being fluent in seven different languages.

So, even though it's easier to be loud than it is to be quiet, I commit to try harder to obey the Apostle Paul and study to be quiet, as well as to be fluent in silence.

Maybe you should stop trying to get over it and keep walking through it.

Life goes better when you do not put anything toxic in you nor have anyone toxic around you.

The best way to not be disillusioned is to stop having illusions.

People that continuously tell others to *get lost* are usually screaming, "Help me get found."

While I believe in standing up for what is right, I do not feel that holding up a sign in front of an abortion clinic is the best method of evangelism. Jesus said that signs would follow us, so we don't need to hold a sign of condemnation. In my opinion, while the mother is on the inside aborting the baby, religion is on the outside aborting the mother. It is okay to go and stand and be a witness, but the signs need to be behind the believer, not just in front of them.

Mark 16:20
And they went forth, and preached every where, the Lord working with them, and confirming the word

with *signs following.*

You can never do CPR on time that you kill.

If you are *scared* of getting *scarred*, you will be *scarred* for life, worrying about what you didn't do that you were scared to try.

People can only push your buttons if you give them the remote.

It's amazing how you can be in a great mood, and out of nowhere, the actions of someone else can change everything. Suddenly, your buttons are pushed, and you begin to reel from the way they made you feel.

But, it doesn't have to be that way. When you know who you are and what your purpose is, no one should be able to control your feelings. Keep your remote in your pocket. Then if the channel is changed, it's because you pushed the buttons.

Things will always sit better with you if you can kneel and pray over the things you can't stand.

Arrogance is nothing more than *ignorance* on steroids.

Proverbs 16:18
Pride goeth before destruction, and an haughty spirit before a fall.

People who daily keep up with *Jesus* don't have time to keep up with the *Jones*es.

You can't help being *attacked*, but you can help getting *attached*.

Just after the shipwreck in Acts 27, Paul and his companions found themselves on an island of barbarous people. Trying to warm everyone, Paul gathered some sticks and built a fire. Once the fire heated up, a venomous viper came out of the fire, attacked Paul, and attached itself to Paul's hand. Paul simply shook it off in the fire.

What should have killed him didn't because he did not allow what attacked him to stay attached to him. Too many people in Christianity get attached to things that they are attacked by. Today, I invite you to shake it off!

Acts 28:3
And when Paul had gathered a bundle of sticks, and laid them on the fire, there came a viper out of the

heat, and fastened on his hand

And he shook off the beast into the fire, and felt no harm.

That moment when you find out that Easy Street has potholes.

When God calls the shots, nobody gets wounded.

When life throws you a curve, it won't hit you if you're walking straight.

The Constitution was written by man and can be amended by man. The Bible was written by God and cannot be amended by man. There can never be an amendment to His commandments.

Sometimes memory is not a *lane*; it's a *pain*.
It is imperative that you choose what to remember and what to forget.

Philippians 3:13
Brethren, I count not myself to have apprehended: but this one thing I do, forgetting those things which are

behind, and reaching forth unto those things which
are before,

You have to pass the past test.

If you can't get past your past, the School Master can't pro-
mote you to your future. I would highly recommend that you
treat your past the same way that Jesus did. He cast it as far as
the east is from the west. He cast it into the sea.

Now, if you can do that too, you would be surprised at how
fast you'll find your future.

Here it is in a nutshell: Once you get past your past, you'll
find your future, fast.

Don't allow *some* people to be the *sum* of how you char-
acterize all people.

Your future was never meant to be a twin of your past. Born
at two separate times, your past is old; your future is new.

Hearing God's voice is a choice. Take Him off mute, and
put Him on speaker.

It's not that you tried to leave someone out. The time just came that you had to weed them out.

When it comes to your core friend group, be careful who you include in your inner circle.

Connecting to the light without disconnecting from the dark is impossible.

If you live in the light, you don't have to worry about dying in the dark.

Too many temporary fixes can make you a permanent fixer.

Sometimes the struggle is not how to *connect* the *dots*; it's how to *disconnect* from the *dysfunction*.

Don't spend so much time reviewing yesterday and pre-viewing tomorrow that you miss the view of today.

It's easier to teach your *dog* to *shake* than it is to teach your *mouth* to *shut*.

Just because you don't *understand* a person, you have no right to say you *can't stand* them.

You don't have to *adopt* everyone else's views, but you need to learn to *adapt* to views other than your own.

When you have the mind of Christ, you don't mind being His hands and feet too.

Don't allow *conflict* to cause you to *inflict* words on others that will *afflict* them.

"The sky is the limit" only applies to people with limited knowledge. One of the fundamental beliefs of Christianity is Heaven. I do believe that Heaven is higher than the sky.

If I take responsibility for what I say and how I said it, I need you to take responsibility for how you understood it.

Whatever you are *expending* your energy on needs to be *expanding* your horizons.

When you feel the urge to *quit*, try to find a *quiet* place first. From my experience, the *quiet* always stops the urge to *quit*.

Some people struggle with *weight*, while others struggle with *wait*. As someone who has experienced both, the struggle is real. Both require patience to change.

Unless you are reporting live from someone's heart, be careful of the news story that you print. Someone is sure to believe your press release even though you weren't present.

If you start looking at the *waves* and stop listening to the *Word*, you will sink. Ask Peter.

Matthew 14: 28-31

And Peter answered him and said, Lord, if it be thou, bid me come unto thee on the water. And he said, Come. And when Peter was come down out of the ship, he walked on the water, to go to Jesus. But when he saw the wind boisterous, he was afraid; and beginning to sink, he cried, saying, Lord, save me. And immediately Jesus stretched forth his hand, and caught him, and said unto him, O thou of little faith, wherefore didst thou doubt?

When searching for a church, you need to be more concerned about their *THEOLOGY* than their *TECHNOLOGY*.

There is certainly nothing wrong with having the latest *technology*, but there is something wrong with having the newest *Theology*.

A *misconception* of God will make you *miss* the *conception* of God's will.

It's great to stand on God's *promises*, but it's also great to sit on His *premises*.

Hebrews 10:25
Not forsaking the assembling of ourselves together,
as the manner of some is; but exhorting one another:
and so much the more, as ye see the day approaching.

You can't walk in God's blessings if you are always blessing others out.

Instead of praying for fewer problems, we need to pray for more power.

Don't let anyone talk you out of doing what God talked you into doing.

Life works a lot better when you work too.

2 Thessalonians 3:10
For even when we were with you, this we commanded
you, that if any would not work, neither should he eat.

Usually, the people that don't *understand* you will try to *undermine* you.

Fake friends use you as a ladder to stand on. True friends use you as a shoulder to lean on.

An *ego trip* usually always ends in the *fall*.

Proverbs 16:18 Pride goes before destruction, a haughty spirit before a fall.

In Matthew 7, Jesus talks about those who build on the sand versus those who build on the rock. It doesn't matter how many lines you draw in the sand, flood waters will eventually wash that line away. Whatever it is that you are building today, set it in stone. It's worth the extra effort in the long run.

My goal as a Christian is not to be in the *limelight*. It's to be in the city where the *Lamb* is the *light*.

Rev. 21:23
And the city had no need of the sun, neither of the moon, to shine in it: for the glory of God did lighten

it, and the Lamb is the light thereof.

Most problems don't *dissolve*. You have to work to make them *resolve*.

I have never had to eject from a *plane*, but I have had to eject from a *plan*. If my plans do not coincide with God's plans, it's parachute time!

It's hard to hold a grudge and hold your peace at the same time.

> Exodus 14:14
> The Lord shall fight for you, and ye shall hold your peace.

The best way to keep people from seeing your *good aptitude* is a *bad* attitude.

I've found that my attitude has a lot to do with my altitude. When I lift my eyes to the Lord and look heavenward, I'm fine. But, when I hang my head and look down at my circumstances, my demeanor is lowered.

Today, I choose to look up!

Your *response* on social media was read. Now, take *responsibility* and change the things you don't like.

I invite every Christian that has a social media account to reread 2 Chronicles 7:14.

It does not say:

If my people who are called by my name, will arrogantly get on social media and blast sinners, and seek their agenda, and turn sinners farther away from Christ, then will I hear from heaven, and will forgive their sin and heal their land.

It reads:

If my people, which are called by my name, shall humble themselves, and pray, and seek my face, and turn from THEIR wicked ways; then will I hear from heaven, and will forgive their sin, and heal their land.

Let's spend our energy praying for our country!

People that have the most successful businesses are people that mind their own.

I've heard it said that for every new *level*, there is a new *devil*.

I choose to say that for every new *phase*, there is a new *praise*.

In 1748, Benjamin Franklin wrote an article that he called, "Advice to a Young Tradesman, Written by an Old One."

While the whole article is worth the read, most of us have heard one of the phrases that he coined in this publication. He said that time is money, and I have to agree.

Every day, we spend our time on whatever we choose. Since Franklin's statement is true, TIME has to be treated as an investment. We have to know where to deposit it to get the best return, as well as when to withdraw it.

There is a super thin line between knowing who or what is a withdrawal of your time and who or what is a deposit of your time. When you exit this life, you may leave money for others to spend, but you will not leave one minute of time for someone else to enjoy.

Time is money. Invest it wisely.

If you give the same credence to the praise of your friends as you do the criticism of your enemies, you should always be at an even keel.

The more time you spend *preparing*, the less time you will have to spend *repairing*.

Don't put your *trust* in things that *rust*.

Matthew 6:19-20
Lay not up for yourselves treasures upon earth, where
moth and rust doth corrupt, and where thieves break
through and steal. But lay up for yourselves treasures
in heaven, where neither moth nor rust doth corrupt,
and where thieves do not break through nor steal:

Sometimes a word of advice is better than a book of
correction.

Proverbs 11:14
Where no counsel is, the people fall: but in the multitude of counsellors there is safety.

Proverbs 15:10
Correction is grievous unto him that forsaketh the
way: and he that hateth reproof shall die.

Balance is the ability to color inside the lines while you
think outside the box.

The best antidote to not being caught up in a dog-eat-dog-
world is not to be a dog.

Philippians 3:2
Beware of dogs, beware of evil workers, beware of the concision.

Setting something in stone is better than drawing a line in the sand.

Revelation 2:17
Whoever has ears, let them hear what the Spirit says to the churches. To the one who is victorious, I will give some of the hidden manna. I will also give that person a white stone with a new name written on it, known only to the one who receives it.

Tasting the blood from biting your lip is better than tasting the blunder of eating your words.

Psalm 34:13
Keep thy tongue from evil, and thy lips from speaking guile.

Life is a mixture of sitting on the shore waiting for your ship to come in and sitting on the ship waiting to get back to shore.

If you are an animal, go along with the HERD.

If you are a human, don't go along with something you HEARD.

Usually, a *knot* in your stomach is a *not* in your spirit.

After you deal with the *root* of the problem, you'll find the *route* to the promise.

Great *peace* is better than great *pace*. Slow down and enjoy life!

As someone who has somewhat of a "hyper" personality, rushing is just normal for me. Going wide open all of the time has become a part of my personality. However, with age, I am "slowly" learning that life is not all about pace; it's all about peace.

Don't call *coincidence* the thing that God calls *providence*.

There are some things that I think.

There are some things that I know.
There are some things that I think that I know.
But there are some things I know that I know!

Job 19:25
For I know that my Redeemer lives, and that he shall
stand at the latter day upon the earth.

2 Timothy 1:12
For the which cause I also suffer these things: nevertheless I am not ashamed: for I know whom I have
believed, and am persuaded that he is able to keep that
which I have committed unto him against that day.

The best way to *gauge* the will of God is to *engage* in the
Word of God.
You will never find His will if you don't find time to
read His Word.

Don't let someone's misrepresentation of God be the catalyst by which you judge Jesus and the rest of us who are gen-
uinely trying to represent Him well.
Not everyone that *represents* Him *resembles* Him.
Humans err; God doesn't.

It's great to save money as long as you know that money can't save you.

1 Peter 1:18-19
Forasmuch as ye know that ye were not redeemed with corruptible things, as SILVER and GOLD, from your vain conversation received by tradition from your fathers; But with the precious blood of Christ, as of a lamb without blemish and without spot:

As a Christian, I should be able to disagree with someone and not "dis" them.
Christian maturity is when you can disagree with someone without disrespecting them.

There is never a *good excuse* for someone to give you a *bad experience*.

Use caution when getting something off of your *chest*.
Your words could very well settle deep into someone else's *heart*.

It's very accurate to say that Jesus gives us power against the enemy. But, it's also very accurate to say that the enemy attacks us at our weakest points.

Whether it's your family, Church, workplace, or whatever you are involved in, the devil will create chaos and bring division. Jesus Himself said that the enemy has come to steal, kill, and destroy.

So, whatever you do, keep unity in your lives. A threefold cord, the book of Ecclesiastes says, is not quickly broken. The devil can only devour what he's able to divide.

1 Peter 5:8
Be sober, be vigilant; because your adversary the devil, as a roaring lion, walks about, seeking whom he may devour:

Mark 3:25
And if a house divided against itself, that house cannot stand.

You will never figure life out until you figure God in.

Don't allow the *excess* of natural things to deter you from *access* to spiritual matters.

Hebrews 12:1
Wherefore seeing we also are compassed about with so great a cloud of witnesses, let us lay aside every weight, and the sin which doth so easily beset us, and let us run with patience the race that is set before us,

You will never be able to *defeat* anything if you don't *defend* something.

Don't be blindsided by one-sided opinions.

It's better to have too many *boos* from an enemy than to have too much *booze* with a friend.

Romans 13:13
Let us walk honestly, as in the day; not in rioting and drunkenness, not in chambering and wantonness, not in strife and envying.

Ephesians 5:18
And be not drunk with wine, wherein is excess; but be filled with the Spirit;

One of the signs of a small mind is a big mouth.

A *better future* can only happen when you let go of a *bitter past.*

We all love to quote Jeremiah 29:11: For I know the plans I have for you, declares the Lord, plans to prosper you and not to harm you, plans to give you hope and a future.

I believe this verse with all of my heart. God has a bright future for you. However, your past can play a huge role in your future. Until you get past the bitter things that have happened, you will get stymied in the present because of the past.

To have the future that God says you can have in Jeremiah, you have to also take the advice of Paul in Philippians 3:13: Brothers, I count not myself to have apprehended: but this one thing I do, forgetting those things which are behind, and reaching forth unto those things which are before.

I am all for any counseling, self-help groups, meetings, or groups that can help people. However, if I understand the scripture correctly, when we get forgiveness of our sins, God throws our sins away. He reverses the charges that were against us. I do not think that rehab should be to constantly rehash all of our wrongs.

There should never be a reason to *rehearse* the sins that God has *reversed.*

Your *reputation* is built by *repetition* of doing the right thing over and over and over.

Popular people will eventually lose their popularity, but honorable people never lose their honor.

Honor is more than a *roll*. It's a *role*.

Fake money and fake morals will both catch up with you. For real.

Nothing *superficial* is ever *beneficial* to the Kingdom of God.

You have to be a person with *principle* for people to have an *interest* in your faith.

Acts 24:25
And as he reasoned of righteousness, temperance, and judgment to come, Felix trembled, and answered, Go thy way for this time; when I have a convenient

season, I will call for thee.

2 Timothy 3:17
That the man of God may be perfect, thoroughly fur-
nished unto all good works.

Don't let a *leg you see* impact your *leg-a-cy*.

Matthew 5:28
But I say unto you, That whosoever looketh on a
woman to lust after her hath committed adultery with
her already in his heart.

Transparency will ultimately bring tranquility. When you
are at peace with yourself and who you are, you are not afraid
to be you.

Crooked people never worry about getting their facts straight.

Ethics apply to all ethnicities. No one gets a free pass.
Character is not a cultural thing.

Being *seduced* is the process of being *reduced* to someone that God didn't create you to be.

> 2 Timothy 3:13
> But evil men and seducers shall wax worse and worse, deceiving, and being deceived.

A lot of people want to *say what they do*, but fewer people want to *do what they say*.

Don't do dumb things with your smartphone.

I refuse to *deface* my *character* to *embrace* the *culture*.

In acting, a character is someone you play.
In real life, character is someone you are.
Never confuse the two.

1 Corinthians 15:33

Do not be deceived: "Bad company corrupts good morals."

Problems:

You can't *think* them away.

You can't *drink* them away.

To get them to *stay* away,

you have to *pray* them away.

Chapter 10
Finding Humor in Truth

People are amazing.

They get up every morning, take coffee beans that have been previously ground, and put them into hot water for maximum taste. They drink juice that came from fruit that had to be squeezed to get its flavor. They scramble an egg that is cracked, and then they put the egg into hot oil that was pressed and beaten from an olive.

They then put on perfume made of crushed flowers and put on wool sweaters from the wool of a sheep that had been shorn. Walking out of their house, they put on their leather shoes from a cow that died for the use of its hide.

Everything about their lives required something drastic to happen beforehand, and yet people whine about every little thing that makes them uncomfortable.

I was raised in a church where we took prayer requests. A very popular request was, "Pray for my *unsaved loved ones*."

With that being a little hard to say, sometimes we also prayed for someone's *unloved saved ones.*

That moment when you're asked to pray for someone with "very close veins." (Or was it varicose veins?)

In the South, when you hear someone say, "I'm fixing to do something," just brace yourself. Ain't nothing getting fixed.

Middle age is that time that you stop trying to get *buff* and try to get to a *buffet.*

I'm that guy, the one that if someone asks me for a *toast,* I make sure they have *jelly too.*

That moment you smile when you hear your wife in the next room saying, "You are perfect in all of your ways." Then, you realize she's singing, "Good, Good, Father."

If all you do is spread God's word, you never have to eat your own.

Most of the time, LOL should be LAL (Lying about laughing).

I'm not trying to start a debate, but I wonder if November 1st ever confuses kids.

That's the day parents put the kids' devil costumes in the closet and bring out their angel wings for the Christmas play.

As a Minister, I study Greek extensively, but I still can't say *gyro* at the sandwich shop.

Hands-down that was the best thumbs-up ever.

Don't be surprised if the big picture of your life does not contain all of your selfies.

Life has a funny way of taking you from a *weight* bench at the gym to the *wait* bench at the mall.

Skinny people can still have a wait problem.

God gave the plan, but Noah was the first ARK-A-TECH.

According to scientific data, the body has 100 billion nerves. It takes a really obnoxious person to be able to get on all of them, but it has happened.

When you think that someone is marriage material, remember this:

When a man hears *material*, he thinks about *studs* and *steel*.

When a woman hears *material*, she thinks about *satin* and *silk*.

If you are a Christian, you understand the analogy of Jesus being the Shepherd and we being His sheep. So, you will understand when I say that the Shepherd loves *ewe*.

If you're not a Christian, He loves *you* too.

Eve was the only person that told the truth when she said to Adam, "Everyone is doing it."

Because my mother was a seamstress, I now get to rip what she sewed.

One of my pet peeves is a healthy man that won't get a job, yet, because he's broke, he wants you to feel he's persecuted like Job.

There is no *margarine* for error, *Butter* Galloway

I gauge my jokes as really good when they get a drum roll and an eye roll.

My generation missed a magnificent moment in time. We could have been taking selfies all of these years because we had a Polaroid camera. It never dawned on us back in the day that we could turn our bathroom into a photography studio. It grieves me to think of how many selfies I missed because we were taught that cameras were meant to take pictures of others. Oh well, you live and learn. I'll let it be a lesson to selfie.

Nobody accepts responsibility anymore. Even when a robber was caught with someone else's safe, his response was, "It's not my *VAULT*."

Do you think that Quakers ever sowed wild oats?

When some people sing, they have *synthesizers*; when I sing, I have *sympathizers*.

That moment when the preacher reads this text from the book of Psalms, and you think there is a possibility of a short sermon.

He reads, "One thing have I desired of the Lord."

You say, "Yes! One thing!"

Then he declares, "For the next little while, I want to talk to you about twelve things you need to do in order to have one particular thing."

45 minutes later...

If there is no Easter bunny, why are there so many Church hoppers?

When an older person is *kneading dough*, they are making bread.

When a young person is *needing dough*, they want money.

While waiting in a long bank line, it was finally my turn. The teller apologized and said, "Sorry about your wait."

I said, "No problem, but I have lost ten pounds."

Then, of course, I had to explain the difference between wait and weight.

I called a local restaurant to order some food for takeout. When I arrived, the lady said, "Do you have a pickup?"

I said, "Yes, but I am in my car today, why?"

My only pet is a peeve;
It doesn't bark, meow, or oink. It just sighs.

If you are a teacher, do you need an *eye* phone to call your *pupils*?

Don't get too excited when someone tells you that you are sweet. One day you're a lifesaver, and the next day you're a sucker. But, you're still sweet.

Wrinkles are nothing more than a sign that people have spent a lot of their life trying to iron things out.

I don't have a food allergy, but I do have a food analogy:

As men we all want to be the top banana. Usually, we are nothing more than an egghead that brings home the bacon. We try to butter up our spouses, and be as sweet as molasses, and act as if life is a piece of cake. Sometimes life is one tough cookie that you have to take with a grain of salt. But I refuse to let one bad apple make me have sour grapes. So, I will spill the beans and be a couch potato for a night. Maybe one day I'll be the big cheese, but for now, I'm happy with just being cheesy.

I'm not afraid of change. I've had to roll enough of it that I've learned to roll with it.

Why is it that kids blow kisses and adults blow fuses?

Two-thirds of our church enjoyed the opening song today. Our worship team began with, "He's an on-time God; yes, He is." The other one-third didn't hear it because they weren't on time; no, they weren't.

I asked our Worship leader to please stop singing *Jesus Paid It All* before the offering.

That moment when your six-year-old granddaughter says, "Pappy, I've seen your commercial on TV."
Then she asks, "Why do you say the same thing every time?"

If you had thrown all the money in the bank that you threw in the wishing well, you would not wish you had a little money today.

You know that sweet compliment that someone gave you when they said you were ONE-IN-A-MILLION? That would have been really sweet 6 billion, 999 million people ago.

There's nothing cuter than a kid that needs a Band-Aid for the mildest scratch. But, there's nothing uglier than an adult that follows suit.

Dramamine–The medicine you take when you have to deal with drama queens.

Mommas don't let your babies grow up to be astronauts. No matter who their relationship is with, they will always need a little more space.

Eve lost everything in the garden except for being Abel to raise Cain.

Genesis 4:1-2
And Adam knew Eve his wife; and she conceived, and bare Cain, and said, I have gotten a man from the Lord. And she again bare his brother Abel. And Abel was a keeper of sheep, but Cain was a tiller of the ground.

Why, yes, I am trying to win an award for running. My goal is the *No belly prize*.

If you are a middle-aged Christian and still think Jeremiah was a bullfrog, you should probably sign up for a Bible study.

Don't be so carnal that the Bible does not amaze you, but don't be so spiritual that it does not amuse you. There is some funny stuff in the Bible!

Adam is the only man that ever went to sleep single and woke married.

> Genesis 2:21-22
> And the Lord God caused a deep sleep to fall upon Adam, and he slept: and he took one of his ribs, and closed up the flesh instead thereof; And the rib, which the Lord God had taken from man, made [9] he a woman, and brought her unto the man.

Adam woke up and said, *"WOE, MAN!"* So, he called her *woman*.

Don't worry if you're in a *jam*; God will *preserve* you.

Psalm 16:1
Preserve me, O God: for in thee do I put my trust.

It's evident that people have different tastes in life. I don't get how anyone could like olives or celery. But, I also don't understand how anyone would not like steak, especially WELL DONE.

Yes, I'm the guy that always kindly asks for everything, including chicken and pork as well as beef, to be cooked WELL DONE. Sometimes, I order *extra well done,* just in case. Yes, I go into Wendy's and get the Jr. Cheeseburger, *extra well done*. OH WELL.

Usually, waitresses and cooks look at me strangely, but I like what I like. But then, when you dine with others, and they order their steak rare, it's a real dilemma. I have been known to put a menu up between them and me so I will not see the blood gushing on their plate. I don't think that a meal was meant for the cattle to be lowing still. It's put me in a yucky moooooood.

Anyway, I think that I have Scripture for my taste. The Bible does not say that Jesus will say, "RARE, good and faithful servant."

He will not say, "MEDIUM RARE, good and faithful servant, or MEDIUM, good and faithful servant."

He won't even say, "MEDIUM WELL, good and faithful servant."

He will say, "WELL DONE, good and faithful servant."

Matthew 25:21
His lord said to him, 'Well done, good and faithful servant; you were faithful over a few things, I will make you ruler over many things. Enter into the joy of your lord.'

Sorry if I took that scripture out of context.
I'll have an 8-ounce rib-eye, WELL DONE, please.

Don't be surprised when the *BIG PICTURE* of your life does not contain all of your *SELFIES*.

Do Churches that serve *jelly-filled* donuts serve them so they will have a *jam-packed* crowd?

Chapter 11
Religion v. Relationship

People that are always looking for a *sign* make Jesus *sigh*.

> Mark 8:12
> And he sighed deeply in his spirit, and saith, Why doth
> this generation seek after a sign? verily I say unto you,
> There shall no sign be given unto this generation.

John 13 is one of the most amazing stories in the Bible. Jesus took a basin of water and a towel and washed the feet of His disciples. One by one, each of them had the hands of Jesus touch their feet.

But sadly, Judas left the room with clean feet and a dirty heart. He left that intimate environment and went and sold Jesus for 30 pieces of silver. He had spent almost every day with Jesus for the past three and a half years, but Judas still sold the Savior.

That tells me that you can hang around Jesus and even go to Church. You can be served by the Pastor, the staff, and even Jesus. But, unless you let Jesus clean your heart with His blood, it doesn't matter how clean your feet are or how spiffy you are on the outside.

Christianity is not about looking the part; it's about being the person that Christ has called you to be.

Most people I have met that say they are disenfranchised with religion aren't really disenfranchised with religion.

They are *disenfranchised* with people that have *franchised* religion.

Galatians 1:14
And profited in the Jews' religion above many my equals in mine own nation, being more exceedingly zealous of the traditions of my fathers. I don't know if which is worse, someone who is disenfranchised with their faith or those who make a franchise of their faith.

Matthew 21:12-13
And Jesus went into the temple of God, and cast out all them that sold and bought in the temple, and overthrew the tables of the moneychangers, and the seats of them that sold doves, And said unto them, It is written, My house shall be called the house of prayer; but ye have made it a den of thieves.

The early Church had *prayer meetings* to pull people out of sin.

The modern Church has *interest meetings* to try and pull people out of another Church.

Preachers need to make sure what we say that is *appealing* to people is not *appalling* to God.

> 2 Timothy 4:2-4
> Preach the word; be instant in season, out of season; reprove, rebuke, exhort with all longsuffering and doctrine. For the time will come when they will not endure sound doctrine; but after their own lusts shall they heap to themselves teachers, having itching ears; And they shall turn away their ears from the truth, and shall be turned unto fables.

> 1 Corinthians 2:4
> And my speech and my preaching was not with enticing words of man's wisdom, but in demonstration of the Spirit and of power:

A church should never be measured by how many are in *attendance* in the pews but how many are seeking *repentance* at the altar.

2 Corinthians 7:10
For godly sorrow produces repentance leading to salvation, not to be regretted; but the sorrow of the world produces death.

True Christianity is not a *publicity stun*t; it's a public and a *private stand.*

Ephesians 6:13-14
Wherefore take unto you the whole armor of God that ye may be able to withstand in the evil day, and having done all, to stand. Stand therefore, having your loins girt about with truth, and having on the breastplate of righteousness.

You have to be a person with *principle* for people to have an *interest* in your faith.

Acts 24:25
And as he reasoned of righteousness, temperance, and judgment to come, Felix trembled, and answered, Go thy way for this time; when I have a convenient season, I will call for thee.

2 Timothy 3:17

That the man of God may be perfect, thoroughly fur-
nished unto all good works.

The Church is not a *building* for people to *see;* it's a *body*
for people to *be*.

> 1 Corinthians 6:19
> What? Know ye not that your body is the temple of
> the Holy Ghost which is in you, which ye have of
> God, and ye are not your own?

> Colossians 1:18
> And he is the head of the body, the church: who is
> the beginning, the firstborn from the dead; that in all
> things he might have the preeminence.

God-fearing ministers yearn to hear God say, *"Well done,"*
more than they want to hear people say, *"Well said."*

> 1 Corinthians 2:4
> And my speech and my preaching was not with
> enticing words of man's wisdom, but in demonstra-
> tion of the Spirit and of power.

> Matthew 25:21

His lord said unto him, Well done, thou good and faithful servant: thou hast been faithful over a few things, I will make thee ruler over many things: enter thou into the joy of thy lord.

Religion looks for *"cream of the crop"* Christians that can enhance their cause. The Lord looks for those who have been *cropped down* and feel like they have no cause.

1 Samuel 22:2
And every one that was in distress, and every one that was in debt, and every one that was discontented, gathered themselves unto him; and he became a captain over them: and there were with him about four hundred men.

Galatians 1:14
And profited in the Jews' religion above many my equals in mine own nation, being more exceedingly zealous of the traditions of my fathers.

In a world of *new and improved*, we need something that's *old and approved* by God. The only thing that I can find that meets that criteria is the Bible.

2 Timothy 2:15
Study to show thyself approved unto God, a workman that needs not to be ashamed, rightly dividing the word of truth.

It's amazing how people call a preacher long-winded if he preaches one hour in a *sermon series*, but they say nothing about the four hours of watching a *world series*.

2 Timothy 3:1-5
This know also, that in the last days perilous times shall come. For men shall be lovers of their own selves, covetous, boasters, proud, blasphemers, disobedient to parents, unthankful, unholy, Without natural affection, trucebreakers, false accusers, incontinent, fierce, despisers of those that are good, Traitors, heady, high-minded, lovers of pleasures more than lovers of God; Having a form of godliness, but denying the power thereof: from such turn away.

Beware of people that always *obsess* over the sins of others but never *confess* sins of their own.

Matthew 7:3-5
And why beholdest thou the mote that is in thy brother's eye, but considerest not the beam that is in thine

own eye? Or how wilt thou say to thy brother, Let me pull out the mote out of thine eye; and, behold, a beam is in thine own eye? Thou hypocrite, first cast out the beam out of thine own eye; and then shalt thou see clearly to cast out the mote out of thy brother's eye.

Biting your lip is always better than eating your words.

Job 2:10
But he said to her, "You speak as one of the foolish women speaks. Shall we indeed accept good from God, and shall we not accept adversity?" In all this Job did not sin with his lips.

When you view Christianity as a *revelation*, you spend your time exploring God's Word.

When you view Christianity as a list of *regulations,* you spend your time explaining your works.

You can't *go* to the Kingdom of Heaven without praying, "Thy Kingdom *come* to earth."

Matthew 6:10
Thy kingdom come. Thy will be done in earth, as it
is in heaven.

When the creation tries to become the Creator, all that is
created is chaos.

Romans 1:25
Who changed the truth of God into a lie, and wor-
shipped and served the creature more than the Creator,
who is blessed for ever. Amen.

Grace is when people throw you to the *wolves,*
and you land in the arms of the *Shepherd.*

Jesus had to deal with the devil for a few days, but He had
to deal with religion for His entire ministry.

Religion is more powerful than the devil. The devil tempted
Jesus a short while and left Him alone. Religion tempted Him
daily and never left Him alone. In fact, religion killed Him.

Luke 4:13
And when the devil had ended all the temptation, he
departed from him for a season.

I love the saying, *by heart*. It means that you have committed
something to memory. It has become a part of who you are.

That's interesting because your memory is in your mind
not in your heart.

A relationship with God that is by heart is a much deeper
relationship than one that's only in your head.

Don't get so preoccupied with what you are going through
that you forget where you are going to.

Heaven is a real place!

It's easier for Christians to *move their letter* than it is to
remove their lethargy.

In Genesis 1, God designed man in His image and defined
him by His character.

In Romans 1, man tried to design God in his image, by not
only redesigning themselves but redefining themselves without
character at all.

Until we get back to who God said we are, we will never help others find out who they are supposed to be.

In John, the eighth chapter, religion stood holding stones to stone a sinner woman.

As they "told on" her to Jesus, He stooped and wrote on the ground.

I don't know what He wrote when He stooped, but I do know what He said: "Let him that is without sin, cast the first stone."

From the oldest to the youngest, the people standing with stones dropped them and walked away.

Jesus still stoops, in hopes that we will stop trying to stone people.

You can have knowledge of God without acknowledging Him as your Lord.

Get a telescope and look at God's stars, not a microscope to look at God's people's scars.

The Bible commands each of us to be a *burden-bearer*.
The Bible condemns each of us for being a *tale-bearer*.

Galatians 6:2
Bear ye one another's burdens, and so fulfil the law
of Christ.

1 Peter 4:15
But let none of you suffer as a murderer, or as a
thief, or as an evildoer, or as a busybody in other
men's matters.

Even though *backslider* is a Biblical term, some don't think
it's possible. Even though *backbiter* is a Biblical term, some
don't believe they are ever guilty.

Proverbs 14:14
The backslider in heart shall be filled with his own
ways: and a good man shall be satisfied from himself.

Romans 1:30
Backbiters, haters of God, despiteful, proud, boasters,
inventors of evil things, disobedient to parents,

A church should not be a place that you just *fill the pew*; you
need to *feel the Presence*.

Christianity is not just *reserved* for Sunday. It is intended to *preserve* you every day.

One of the things you should never hear a Christian Pastor say is, "Don't try this at home."

As a Pastor, it makes our job so much easier when people do try this at home. Christianity is not something reserved for Church on Sunday; it is something that preserves your home all of the other days.

Do try this at home!

The religious people of Jesus's day had the ability to *memorize* prophecies, but they didn't have the ability to *recognize* the Prophet when He came.

In Genesis 1, God made man in His image. In Romans 1, man made God in his image. What is wrong with this picture? This is not just a play on words. If God created man in His image, shouldn't the image that man made of God still look like God?

Yes, it really should, but it didn't. It was so far removed from anything that even resembled God. Overall, Romans 1 is as sad as Genesis 1 is happy.

While I won't take the time to dissect and give a commentary on all of this, let me make a couple of points.

God still wants you to reflect His image. He wants you to look like Him, live like Him, and love like Him.

Don't allow the downward spiral of a worldly system to replace an upward desire that God has placed in you.

Let it be said of us as John said in 1 John 3:2, "Beloved now are we the sons of God, and it does not yet appear what we shall be: but we know that when He shall appear we shall be like Him, for we shall see Him as He is."

The original image of how He made us was reestablished the day He saved us!

Zechariah 9:9
Rejoice greatly, Daughter Zion! Shout, Daughter Jerusalem! See, your king comes to you, righteous and victorious, lowly and riding on a donkey.

If Jesus rode on a *lowly donkey*, why are so many Christians riding on a *high horse*?

If Christianity had as many fruit growers as fruit inspectors, there would be no room in the barn for the fruit.

Faith is more than a *profession*; it's a *possession* of the attributes of Christ.

If people spent as much time chasing their *dreams* as they did chasing *drama*, nothing would be impossible.

Make sure that your Christianity is *sacrificial*, not *superficial*.

Romans 12:1
I beseech you therefore, brethren, by the mercies of God, that ye present your bodies a living sacrifice, holy, acceptable unto God, which is your reasonable service.

Royalty is a word that is discussed in a lot of Christian circles. I love the fact that Jesus said we as Christians are a royal priesthood. However, there is no such thing as *royalty* without *loyalty*.

Be true to who you are chosen to be.

To be a *Royal Priest*, you have to be a *Loyal Person*.

1 Peter 2:9
But ye are a chosen generation, a royal priesthood, an holy nation, a peculiar people, that ye should shew forth the praises of him who hath called you out of darkness into his marvellous light:

Galatians 6:1
Brethren, if a man be overtaken in a fault, ye which are spiritual, restore such an one in the spirit of meekness;

considering thyself, lest thou also be tempted.

If this verse is the Biblical pattern for restoring the fallen, why is it not as a much a doctrine of the Church as other things? It seems that faultfinders often overtake those over-taken in a fault.

My prayer is that God would allow me as a Christian to be a *fallen finder* without being a *faultfinder*.

An ego trip will always end in the fall.

Proverbs 16:18
Pride goeth before destruction, and an haughty spirit before a fall.

In a conversation with Jesus, Nicodemus was the first person to hear the most famous of all Bible verses, John 3:16. But Nicodemus left that day without professing a conversion to Christ.

It is possible to have a *conversation* about Christ without experiencing a *conversion* to Christ.

However, the seeds that were sown that day did produce a harvest. Nicodemus was the one that gave Jesus a proper burial, and by doing so, he made a declaration of his faith.

Beware of people that continuously *magnify* the sins of others. That's usually a sign that they have failed to *identify* their own.

The next time you *pencil* God in, remember the *permanent markers* in His hands for you.

Isaiah 49:16
See, I have engraved you on the palms of my hands.

If Christians would stop pointing fingers and start bending knees, we could make a huge difference in our country.

2 Chronicles 7:14
If my people, which are called by my name, shall humble themselves, and pray, and seek my face, and turn from their wicked ways; then will I hear from heaven, and will forgive their sin, and will heal their land.

The only way that Jesus could get His point *across* was to go to *a cross*.

John 19:17
And he bearing his cross went forth into a place called the place of a skull, which is called in the Hebrew Golgotha.

Don't condense God to a Sunday service.
Expand Him into your work week.

People don't want to overhear you speaking *about God* if you won't speak *to them*.

Most people would rather *take a chance* than *make a change*.

With deep regret, the prodigal son made the return home after a rendezvous with wrong. Sadly, his older brother refused to be as accepting of his sibling as the Father was of his son.

When confronted by the Father, the older son gave his dad his résumé of all he had never done.

The Father was faced with one son with regrets of what he had done and one son with a résumé of what he hadn't done. Both had to be forgiven by the same Father.

Today, if you will bring the Father your regrets or your résumé, He will do the same thing with both-throw them away.

The regrets of what we have done and the résumé of what we haven't done call for equal love. And God's love is not swayed by how bad we've been or how good we've been.

The unrighteous and the self-righteous are all saved by the same grace of a loving Father.

An *inclusive Christ* never meant for His Church to be an *exclusive club*.

> Mark 2:15
> And it came to pass, that, as Jesus sat at meat in his house, many publicans and sinners sat also together with Jesus and his disciples: for there were many, and they followed him.

Be careful not to confuse *righteous* with *religious*; they are not synonymous terms.

The error that dreamers often make is telling jealous brothers about their dreams.

They will make sure that your life is a nightmare, while God is fulfilling your dreams.

~ask Joseph

Genesis 37:5-8

And Joseph dreamed a dream, and he told it his brethren: and they hated him yet the more. And he said unto them, Hear, I pray you, this dream which I have dreamed: For, behold, we were binding sheaves in the field, and, lo, my sheaf arose, and also stood upright; and, behold, your sheaves stood round about, and made obeisance to my sheaf. And his brethren said to him, Shalt thou indeed reign over us? or shalt thou indeed have dominion over us? And they hated him yet the more for his dreams, and for his words.

The focus of a Church should never be about the *pretty stained glass;* It should be about *dirty stained souls.*

While there is nothing wrong with nice church buildings, God's Church was never designed to be just a building. His Church is a body of believers that He has washed in His blood. The Bible says that all of us have sinned and come short of the glory of God and that all of our righteousness is as filthy rags.

At Word of Life Church, our focus is for people to bring their "dirty" laundry and give it to the Lord. When they do that, they will hear these words from John 15:3, "Now are ye clean through the word which I have spoken unto you."

Acts 20:28

Take heed therefore unto yourselves, and to all the flock, over the which the Holy Ghost hath made you overseers, to feed the church of God, which he hath purchased with his own blood.

Revelation 1:5
And from Jesus Christ, who is the faithful witness, and the first begotten of the dead, and the prince of the kings of the earth. Unto him that loved us, and WASHED US FROM OUR SINS IN HIS OWN BLOOD.

The Pharisees wanted Jesus out of the picture because the focus was on Him, not them.

It troubles me a little in today's Christianity that the focus is more on us than Jesus.

It's impossible for your hands to be clean if you're always digging up dirt on others.

Jesus washed Judas' *stinky feet*, but Judas would not let Him wash his *stinky heart*.

John 13:12
So after he had washed their feet, and had taken his garments, and was set down again, he said unto them,

Know ye what I have done to you?

Matthew 26:16
And from that time he sought opportunity to betray him.

Sometimes people need a sermon.
Sometimes they need a shoulder.

Chapter 12
Discipleship

We need to let what's inside of us affect what's around us, instead of allowing us what's around us to affect what's inside of us.

> Romans 12: 1-2
> I beseech you therefore, brethren, by the mercies of God, that ye present your bodies a living sacrifice, holy, acceptable unto God, which is your reasonable service. And be not conformed to this world: but be ye transformed by the renewing of your mind, that ye may prove what is that good, and acceptable, and perfect, will of God.

Forgiveness is not just God clearing your name. It's Him giving you His name.

Isaiah 62: 2
The Gentiles shall see your righteousness, And all
kings your glory. You shall be called by a new name,
Which the mouth of the Lord will name.

It's usually not a *fruit* problem but a *root* problem.

Matthew 13:18-21
Therefore hear the parable of the sower: When anyone
hears the word of the kingdom, and does not understand it, then the wicked one comes and snatches
away what was sown in his heart. This is he who
received seed by the wayside. But he who received
the seed on stony places, this is he who hears the
word and immediately receives it with joy; yet he has
no root in himself, but endures only for a while. For
when tribulation or persecution arises because of the
word, immediately he stumbles.

Fasting is not done so *others* will think we are *spiritual*; we
fast because *God* knows that we are *carnal*.

Matthew 6:16-18
Moreover when you fast, be not, as the hypocrites, of
a sad countenance: for they disfigure their faces that
they may appear unto men to fast. Verily I say unto

you, they have their reward. But you, when you fast, anoint your head, and wash your face; that you appear not unto men to fast, but unto your Father which is in secret: and your Father, which sees in secret, shall reward you openly.

The best way to be full of faith is to be faithful.

Luke 16:10
He that is faithful in that which is least is faithful also in much: and he that is unjust in the least is unjust also in much.

Acts 6:8
And Stephen, full of faith and power, did great wonders and miracles among the people.

God-fearing ministers yearn to hear God say "w*ell done*" more than they want to hear people say "*well said*."

1 Corinthians 2:4
And my speech and my preaching was not with enticing words of man's wisdom, but in demonstration of the Spirit and of power.

Matthew 25:21
His lord said unto him, Well done, thou good and faithful servant: thou hast been faithful over a few things, I will make thee ruler over many things: enter thou into the joy of thy lord.

People who are caught up with the *Gospel* do not have time to be caught up in the *gossip*.

1 Timothy 5:13
And withal they learn to be idle, wandering about from house to house; and not only idle, but tattlers also and busybodies, speaking things which they ought not.

Why is it that it's easier to say "RIP" (rest in peace) to the deceased than it is to "LIP" (live in peace) with the living?

Romans 12:18
If it be possible, as much as lies in you, live peaceably with all men.

The best way to get back on your feet is to get back on your knees.

Ephesians 3:14
For this cause I bow my knees unto the Father of our
Lord Jesus Christ.

Jesus and water:
I believe Jesus's first miracle, but I didn't taste it. He turned
the water into wine. I also believe the miracle where Jesus
walked on water, but I didn't see it.

But according to John 4, as a Christian, I have tasted the
Living Water, and it is in me a well; and according to John 7,
rivers of Living Water are flowing out of me.

No, I've never walked on water, but I'm walking with the
Water of Life in me.

People seem to be very happy that Jesus paid the full price
for their sins, but they want a discount on discipleship. It's true
that salvation is free and it is not works based. Jesus died on
the cross and paid your debt of sin.

However, Jesus also taught us that even though salvation is
free, it requires daily discipleship. He wants us to know that we
don't have to die on a cross as He did, but we do have to daily
deny ourselves, take up our cross, and follow Him.

Discipleship merely means to discipline our lives to follow
Him completely. No matter how many websites you visit or how
many churches you try, there are no discounts on discipleship.

Luke 9:23
And he said to them all, If any man will come after me, let him deny himself, and take up his cross daily, and follow me.

Luke 14:27
And whosoever doth not bear his cross, and come after me, cannot be my disciple.

Fisherman spends thousands of dollars on fake bait. These artificial lures have caught a lot of real fish.

Jesus's first disciples were fishermen. After winning them over with miracles of fish, Jesus told them, "From now on, you will catch men."

His message is still the same for us. But how do we "catch" men?

We won't catch too many men with fake bait! Sinners can spot a fake a mile off. What the world needs more than anything is people that are real.

Live bait is always more appealing than fake.

Some things do not need CPR. You do not need to revive old sins.

Romans 7:9
For I was alive without the law once: but when the commandment came, sin revived, and I died.

There are times in life that we all need correction. That's another reason you need a local church with a local body of believers. We only accept *correction* from those we have a *connection* with.

Hebrews 13:17
Obey them that have the rule over you, and submit yourselves: for they watch for your souls, as they that must give account, that they may do it with joy, and not with grief: for that is unprofitable for you.

Long, fulfilling lives come equipped with slow, painful processes.

1 Peter 5:10 And the God of all grace, who called you to his eternal glory in Christ, after you have suffered a little while, will himself restore you and make you strong, firm and steadfast.

Redoing is not an option.

Repenting is.

Problems weren't meant to keep you from your promise. Sometimes, they are intended to get you to it.

> Philippians 1:12, 19
> But I would ye should understand, brethren, that the things which happened unto me have fallen out rather unto the furtherance of the gospel.
> For I know that this shall turn to my salvation through your prayer, and the supply of the Spirit of Jesus Christ,

If you can answer why you started, you'll always question why you're stopping.

Listen carefully today.

It is possible that time will tell you something that years ago you said only time would tell.

The Rich Young Ruler could not get a new *lease* on life because he was not willing to *sell* what he had and give to the poor.

Matthew 19:21
Jesus said unto him, If thou wilt be perfect, go and sell that thou hast, and give to the poor, and thou shalt have treasure in heaven: and come and follow me.

A *constant* prayer life backed the *instant* miracles of Jesus.

1 Thessalonians 5:17
Pray without ceasing.

You may never be like Peter and be asked to *walk on the waves* to meet Jesus. However, all of us have been invited to *walk in the way* with Jesus.

Other gods are not just something you *carve* with your *hands*; they are something you *crave* with your *heart*.

Proverbs 4:23
Above all else, guard your heart, for everything you do flows from it.

It's impossible to turn pro if you don't turn up for practice.

Daniel 1:4
Children in whom was no blemish, but well favored,
and skillful in all wisdom, and cunning in knowledge,
and understanding science, and such as had ability
in them to stand in the king's palace, and whom
they might teach the learning and the tongue of the
Chaldeans.

When people read your lips, they have an unobstructed
view of the library in your heart.

Matthew 15:8
This people draws nigh unto me with their mouth,
and honors me with their lips; but their heart is
far from me.

If you want to know what someone is made of, look at what
they've made it through.

There is an old nursery rhyme that asks this question, "What
are little boys made of?"

It immediately answers the question with, "Frogs and snails
and puppy dog tails, that's what little boys are made of."

Then it asks, "What are little girls made of?"

Again, it answers, "Sugar and spice and everything nice, that's what little girls are made of."

As cute as that is, what I'm made of is determined by what I was made in. Boys and girls were all made in the image of God. Because of that, when you look at someone, you just need to know that what they are made of is determined by what they made it through.

2 Corinthians 11:22-30

Are they Hebrews? so am I. Are they Israelites? so am I. Are they the seed of Abraham? so am I. Are they ministers of Christ? (I speak as a fool) I am more; in labors more abundant, in stripes above measure, in prisons more frequent, in deaths oft. Of the Jews five times received I forty stripes save one. Thrice was I beaten with rods, once was I stoned, thrice I suffered shipwreck, a night and a day I have been in the deep; In journeyings often, in perils of waters, in perils of robbers, in perils by mine own countrymen, in perils by the heathen, in perils in the city, in perils in the wilderness, in perils in the sea, in perils among false brethren; In weariness and painfulness, in watchings often, in hunger and thirst, in fastings often, in cold and nakedness. Beside those things that are without, that which cometh upon me daily, the care of all the churches. Who is weak, and I am not weak? who is offended, and I burn not? If I must needs glory, I will glory of the things which concern mine infirmities.

It's okay to *contemplate* your Christianity but don't *complicate* it.

>2 Corinthians 11:3
>But I fear, lest by any means, as the serpent beguiled Eve through his subtilty, so your minds should be corrupted from the simplicity that is in Christ.

The greatest ministers are not those who preach behind a *pulpit*. It's those that reach for people and *pull* them out of a *pit*.

>Psalm 40:2
>He brought me up also out of an horrible pit, out of the miry clay, and set my feet upon a rock, and established my goings.

Delivering people that were possessed with demons was easy for Jesus. Over and over again, He delivered people who, in turn, confessed Him as Christ. But it seems that it was easier for Him to deliver people possessed with devils than it was to deliver people obsessed with what they possessed.

The Rich Young Ruler is just one example of someone who was so obsessed with what he possessed that he could not confess Jesus to be his Lord.

What about you? Is it possible to have such an obsession with worldly possessions that we never make a confession of our need for Christ?

Like Jesus, I've seen many people delivered from spirits that possessed them but very few delivered from an obsession with possessions.

> Matthew 19:22
> But when the young man heard that saying, he went away sorrowful: for he had great possessions.

Some things in life are temporary, while others are permanent. It is up to us to decide where the emphasis should be. Some things are meant to last for a few days, while some are meant to endure for a few months. But then, some things are meant to last forever.

Today would be a good day to decide that you will not let temporary things become permanent, but you should also decide to not allow those things that are meant to be permanent to be temporary.

God is waiting on you to stop improvising and to accept what He has already provided.

As Abraham walked in obedience to offer his son as a sacrifice, Isaac observed all of the details were ready except for one thing. He looked at his Father and said, "I see everything except the sacrifice."

Abraham opened his mouth and prophesied, "God will provide Himself a Lamb."

This story turns out good because Abraham walked in total obedience and waited for what God had already provided, even though he couldn't see it.

As I pondered this passage this morning, I couldn't help but think how so many people now have no patience to wait for what God has already provided. Because we are so accustomed to a "now" mentality, we improvise, instead of waiting on God to provide.

This scenario happens in churches as well as homes. But I promise you that there is nothing you can improvise that will fulfill your need like what God has already provided for your life.

It's not your job to throw something together when Jesus has already laid down His life. He is still JEHOVAH-JIREH, my provider!

The only way to *refrain* from *sin* is to be *reformed* by the *Son*.

Whether you use your *sail* to come in *fast* or you crawl like a *snail* and come in *last*, keep moving.

Ecclesiastes 9:11
I returned, and saw under the sun, that the race is not to the swift, nor the battle to the strong, neither yet bread to the wise, nor yet riches to men of understanding, nor yet favor to men of skill; but time and

330

chance happens to them all.

Your *reputation* is built on your *repetition* of what you do daily.

Before Lot's wife had ever turned her head, sin had already turned her heart.

Proverbs 4:23
Guard your heart above all else, for it determines the course of your life.

Luke 17:32
Remember Lot's wife.

Your most significant test of fulfilling your *appointment* given to you from *God* is your ability not to be deterred by your *disappointment* from *people*.

True worship is more than music to your ears; it's meant as a message to your heart.

Who would have dreamed a few years ago that I would be writing this devotion from the palm of my hand?

According to Pew Research, 92% of Americans have a Smartphone of some sort that they place in their palm.

Personally, the phone in the palm of my hand is much more than a phone:

I have my Bible in the palm of my hand.

I have my datebook in the palm of my hand.

I have my camera in the palm of my hand.

I have my photo album in the palm of my hand.

I have instant access to the world in the palm of my hand.

I have my alarm clock in the palm of my hand.

I have my stopwatch in the palm of my hand.

I have my phone book in the palm of my hand.

I have my address book in the palm of my hand.

I have my stereo in the palm of my hand.

I have my TV in the palm of my hand.

I have my calculator in the palm of my hand.

I have my level in the palm of my hand.

I have my flashlight in the palm of my hand.

I have my instruction manual in the palm of my hand.

I can do my banking in the palm of my hand.

On and on I could go, but the point of this is simple. We have so much more in our hands than Jesus did. The only thing He had in the palm of His hand was a nail with a note to you.

Isaiah 49:16
See, I have engraved you on the palms of my hands.

Make sure that what you have in the palm of your hand represents what He had in His!

Your *assignment* to do *God's will* can only be fulfilled through your *alignment* with *God's Word*.

It's tragic when people drink the Kool-Aid of a *religious cult*. But, it's just as bad when people drink the Kool-Aid of a *non-religious culture*.

You are not called to straighten people out. You are called to strengthen people in love.

No, I do not think that Christians should get a *chip in their hand*.
Neither do I not think that Christians should have a *chip on their shoulder*.

Don't allow someone else's erroneous portrait of Christ to skew the way that you are supposed to portray Him.

You are where you are because of where you've been. Nothing can change that. But, if you don't like where you are, you can still get to where you are supposed to be because you now know where you are.

A non-swimmer is safer *surfing the waves* than a non-disciplined person is *surfing the web*.

Prayer doesn't always stop your problems, but it always starts your power.

What keeps us on our knees will also keep us on our toes.

Jesus is not just something you say; He's Someone you call.

I do not believe in complicating Christianity. The simplicity that is found in Christ is easily understood by children. However, it's vital to differentiate things from time to time.

Christ made becoming a Christian so easy. The Bible says that whosoever shall call on the name of the Lord shall be saved.

But, it also says that not everyone that says, "Lord, Lord," will enter into His Kingdom. Call His name, and call upon Him to save you.

> Romans 10:13
> For whosoever shall call upon the name of the Lord shall be saved.

> Matthew 7:21
> Not every one that says unto me, Lord, Lord, shall enter into the kingdom of heaven; but he that doeth the will of my Father which is in heaven.

I'm not afraid of what lies before me. I'm afraid of what I put before God that keeps me from what's before me.

The most famous verse of the Bible is John 3:16:

For God so loved the world that He gave His only begotten Son, that whosoever believes in Him, should not perish, but have everlasting life.

However, not as many people know Matthew 21:22:

And all things, whatsoever you shall ask in prayer, believing, you shall receive.

Whosoever believes on Jesus can have *whatsoever* else they believe through prayer!

When the curtain closes on your life, all that matters is who you were behind the scenes.

Your *identity* will get you into a lot of places. Your *integrity* will keep you out of some.

Tests don't stop when you graduate from college. At every turn of life, there will be tests.

Speaking of tests, I have no trouble with true or false. I'm also reasonably good at multiple choice. But my biggest struggle is knowing how to fill in the blanks.

When I draw a blank, I have to depend on God to fill that void.

When your teacher is pain, the answers are plain.

How you *behave* is a direct correlation to what you *believe*.

You are not in the witness protection program. Christ did not save you for you to be an incognito Christian with an alias name, so He empowered you with His ageless name: Jesus!

You are supposed to *restore the fallen* not *report the fault*.

The Bible says that David danced before the Lord with all of his might. The scripture also says that David was a man after God's own heart.

That simply tells me that God gauges what you do before Him in order to see what you are really after.

The reason God wants no other gods before Him is so you will not go after what you put *before*.

Today, I choose for my *before* and my *after* to please the one true God.

Tomorrow is not a *given*; make sure you are *forgiven* today.

A church is not just a place to *behold the wonder*; it is a place to *befriend the wanderer*.

Yes, your *morality* will affect your *mortality*.

I recently saw someone wearing a t-shirt that read, "Get Lost." I wish so badly that my t-shirt read, "Get Found."

I was born lost, but the Lord found me. People don't need to get lost; they need to get found.

When you *believe*, you will be saved. When you are saved, you *belong* to Christ. When you belong to Christ, you will *become* like Him. When you become like Christ, you will *behold* Him in all of His glory.

You can't control all of the things that are happening around you. But, you can control the things that are happening within you.

When you are blessing the Lord with all that is within you, you will not have time to stress over all that's happening around you!

Psalm 103:1

Bless the Lord, O my soul: and all that is within me, bless his holy name.

The answer to the *downward spiral* of sin is an *upward desire* for the Savior.

338

The struggle is real: But so is the strength that the struggle produces.

2 Corinthians 12:9
And he said unto me, My grace is sufficient for you: for my strength is made perfect in weakness.

I guess you never get too old to experience wanting to be accepted.
Ask Christ. He's wanted everyone to accept Him for the last 2000 years,

Even if you are *filthy rich*, your righteousness is as *filthy rags*.

Isaiah 64:6
But we are all as an unclean thing, and all our righteousnesses are as filthy rags and we all do fade as a leaf; and our iniquities, like the wind, have taken us away.

Being a Christian is more than giving an acceptance speech when you elect Jesus as your Savior. You are accepting a new walk as well as a new talk.

You become a new creation in Christ and speak an entirely new language when you make Him your Lord.

Jesus is not a multiple choice. He's the only answer in a world full of questions.

The world does not need to be Americanized; they need to be Christianized.

In fact, America needs to be Christianized.

God does not give you power just for you to say you have power.

He never gives you power without giving you a purpose for using it.

Acts 1:8

But ye shall receive power, after that the Holy Ghost is come upon you: and ye shall be witnesses unto me both in Jerusalem, and in all Judaea, and in Samaria, and unto the uttermost part of the earth.

Psalm 119:2
Blessed are they that keep his testimonies, and that
seek him with their whole heart.

The *hole* in your *heart* can only be healed when it is filled
by seeking God with your *whole heart*.

Most of the time when you hear people say that you reap
what you sow, it's in a condescending, condemning voice.
However, these powerful words apply to whether you do good
or act badly.

There is a positive side to these words that we need to
declare with our voice. A prime example is found in Psalm
126:5, "They that sow in tears shall reap in joy."

Good or bad, you reap what you sow.

For you to *abound* with Christ in your life, you have to
abide in Him.

Sometimes you don't need a change of heart;
You need to change hearts.

God performed the first heart transplant, and He does thousands of them daily.

1 Samuel 10:9
God gave him another heart.

You may shorten your church service, but you can never shorten your Christian service.

Christian service is 24/7.

I love the verse that says in due season we will reap if we faint not. But, due season will only come if you do what you are supposed to during the other seasons.

Gossip is for the birds! Any ol' parrot can repeat something.

If you live your life with what might have been instead of what will be, your life will always be what might have been.

When you know who you are in Christ, you do not have to listen to other people's *rendition* of your *definition*.

You are who Christ says you are, not what others heard you are.

All of us would love to do something to *astound*, but all God asks of us is to take *a stand*.

Ephesians 6:14
Stand therefore, having your loins girt about with truth, and having on the breastplate of righteousness.

You will never have *preservation* without *perseverance*.

2 Timothy 4:18
And the Lord shall deliver me from every evil work, and will preserve me unto his heavenly kingdom: to whom be glory for ever and ever. Amen.

In order for life to be *amazing*, sometimes you have to make it *amusing*.

Sometimes the race is amusing, but God's grace is always amazing.

When you have the mind of Christ, you have easy access to His ear.

Philippians 2:5
Let this mind be in you, which was also in Christ Jesus:

Isaiah 59:1
Behold, the Lord's hand is not shortened, that it cannot save; neither his ear heavy, that it cannot hear:

The disciples that lived in Jesus's day were *eyewitnesses*. You and I are *ear witnesses*.

2 Peter 1:16
For we have not followed cunningly devised fables, when we made known unto you the power and coming of our Lord Jesus Christ, but were eyewitnesses of his majesty.

Romans 10:17
So then faith cometh by hearing, and hearing by the word of God.

Your neglect of reading the Word of God doesn't negate your responsibility to abide by it.

Hebrews 2:3
How shall we escape, if we neglect so great salvation; which at the first began to be spoken by the Lord, and

was confirmed unto us by them that heard him.

By nature, I am very passive. I hate conflict and discord of any kind. Without trying to sound "too spiritual," I have always tried to excel in the verses where Jesus taught to turn the other cheek.

But one day, it dawned on me that this same Jesus who turned the other cheek also turned over tables in the temple.

I realized that I had to learn the balance in life between when to turn the other cheek and when to turn over the tables.

Matthew 5:39
But I say unto you, That ye resist not evil: but whosoever shall smite thee on thy right cheek, turn to him the other also.

Matthew 21:12
And Jesus went into the temple of God, and cast out all them that sold and bought in the temple, and overthrew the tables of the moneychangers, and the seats of them that sold doves,

You are not allowed to have carry-on baggage on your flight to heaven.

Hebrews 12:1-2
Wherefore seeing we also are compassed about with so great a cloud of witnesses, let us lay aside every weight, and the sin which doth so easily beset us, and let us run with patience the race that is set before us, Looking unto Jesus the author [1] and finisher of our faith; who for the joy that was set before him endured the cross, despising the shame, and is set down at the right hand of the throne of God.

The Christian life is like tennis: everyone gets a chance to serve.

Galatians 5:13
For, brethren, ye have been called unto liberty; only use not liberty for an occasion to the flesh, but by love serve one another.

An altar call is a chance to make *amends* before the *amen*.

Repentance is not repeating a prayer after a Preacher but repenting of my sins before God.

We need more than a *response* to the world's problems. We need to take *responsibility* for the changes that we can make.

You never have to worry about the devil trying to *possess* you if you never let him *impress* you.

2 Corinthians 11:3
But I fear, lest by any means, as the serpent beguiled Eve through his subtilty, so your minds should be corrupted from the simplicity that is in Christ.

Too many relationships are joined at the hip. God intended for you to be joined at the heart.

The rich young ruler was under the influence of affluence.

1 Timothy 6:10
For the love of money is the root of all evil: which while some coveted after, they have erred from the faith, and pierced themselves through with

many sorrows.

America is the country where everyone has a *response* on social media, but very few want to take *responsibility* in real life.

When Jesus hung on the cross, He had thieves on both sides. He didn't choose sides on who to save. Both sides had the same opportunity. Both of them were on the side of the Savior, but only one decided to ask for help.

Matthew 27:38
Then were there two thieves crucified with him, one on the right hand, and another on the left.

Luke 23:39-43
And one of the malefactors which were hanged railed on him, saying, If thou be Christ, save thyself and us. But the other answering rebuked him, saying, Dost not thou fear God, seeing thou art in the same condemnation? And we indeed justly; for we receive the due reward of our deeds: but this man hath done nothing amiss. And he said unto Jesus, Lord, remember me when thou comest into thy kingdom. And Jesus said unto him, Verily I say unto thee, To day shalt thou be with me in paradise.

The early disciples were accused of turning the world upside down. I, along with hundreds of other preachers, have preached this: Let's turn the world upside down for Christ!

However, when you look at this, it was unbelievers who were saying that about Christians. Truthfully, the Christian message was turning the world back right side up. Sin had turned it upside down.

In a day when sin has become the norm, even among Christians, I believe it's time that the church makes a concerted effort to turn the world back right side up for Jesus!

Acts 17:6
And when they found them not, they drew Jason and certain brethren unto the rulers of the city, crying, These that have turned the world upside down are come hither also;

According to the Bible, the primary job of a Pastor is to feed the Church of God. You should always leave Church full on Sunday and have enough left over to "take out."

The people that you rub shoulders with Monday through Saturday need you to leave a good taste in their mouth about what you say you experienced at Church.

Christianity gives you the awesome opportunity to step up to the plate and follow Jesus. It also gives you the opportunity to step back from the plate to follow him by denying yourself with prayer and fasting.

Mark 9:29
And he said unto them, This kind can come forth by nothing, but by prayer and fasting.

You are never allowed to leave the school of hard knocks. After you have finished being the student, you become the teacher, showing others that they can make it.

Like the picture on the puzzle box, most of us know how we think our life is supposed to look. However, some people would rather leave the pieces in the box than to take the time to "get it together."

God wants to help you put your life together. He knows what the big picture of your completed life is supposed to look like.

All He needs you to do is take the pieces out of the box- that place that has become your comfort zone of disconnected pieces.

Then, He will help you. But He will not do it for you; He will do it with you.

So, go ahead today and get out of the box. You will be amazed at the peace you will experience as you allow God to connect your life, piece by piece.

Looking back, you will not see the cards you were dealt but the cross where you knelt.

I love it when a premature baby fully develops. I hate it when an immature adult doesn't.

Psalm 91 is one of my favorite passages of scripture. It begins by saying, "He who dwells in the secret place of the Most High shall abide under the shadow of the Almighty."

If the Almighty is continually moving, that means the secret place is moving too. For the secret place to stay secret, you have to move with the Almighty on a daily basis.

Because I was born that way, I need to be born again this way.

1 Peter 1:23
For you have been born again, not of perishable seed, but of imperishable, through the living and enduring word of God.

Prayer and fasting are not meant to be a *public announcement* of my spirituality; they are intended to be a *private denouncement* of my flesh.

To have power in public, you must have prayer in private.

Prayer is not designed to help you feel better; it is intended to help you live better.

Don't be upset by those who are *finding favor* if you are busy *finding fault*.

The only things that will last are the things you put first.

Matthew 6:33
But seek ye first the kingdom of God, and his righteousness; and all these things shall be added unto you.

Answers to *instant prayers* are usually backed up by a *constant prayer life*.

This generation needs to be taught how to do two things: plead the blood of the Lamb and pledge allegiance to the flag.

People don't just need a shoulder to cry on; they need a confidant to rely on.

Part of my calling is to restore people who fall, no matter how many times they have fallen. However, there comes a time that people need to stop falling and start helping others who have fallen.

Jude 1:24
Unto Him who is able to keep you from falling.

Your fall potential can stymie your full potential.

Sometimes moving forward and holding yourself back are synonymous terms.

If you are an animal, go along with the *herd*.
If you are a human, don't go along with something you *heard*.

Coming in *last* is fine. Just don't come in *lost*.

A mark of Christian maturity is not to take the hurt that is happening to you and hurt others. As hard as it seems, you can take your hurt and help others.

Typically, the value of a house *appreciates* over time, and the price of a vehicle *depreciates* over time. So that must mean that *how you live* is more important than *how you roll*.

As a person who knows without question that I am saved, I never want to be so self-righteous that I won't say the "sinners" prayer. If the great Apostle Paul had to die daily to his flesh, I daily need to smite my chest and say, "Lord, have mercy on me, a sinner."

If you have indeed accepted Christ as your Savior, you have to accept me as your brother.

1 John 4:20
If a man say, I love God, and hates his brother, he is
a liar: for he that loves not his brother whom he hath

seen, how can he love God whom he hath not seen?

People that live a life that *exalts* who God is will never have to *explain* who they are.

Instead of going on a rant about all that is wrong in the world, take a few minutes to read what's right in the Word.

It does not matter *where* you worship, but it does matter *Who* you worship.

John 4:21-24
Jesus saith unto her, Woman, believe me, the hour cometh, when ye shall neither in this mountain, nor yet at Jerusalem, worship the Father. Ye worship ye know not what: we know what we worship: for salvation is of the Jews. But the hour cometh, and now is, when the true worshippers shall worship the Father in spirit and in truth: for the Father seeks such to worship him. God is a Spirit: and they that worship him must worship him in spirit and in truth.

As I sit here watching a football game on television, Denver just got penalized for having too many men on the field. Oh, how I wish we had that problem in the church. Most ministries that I am familiar with do not have enough people in the field.

Jesus told us to lift our eyes to the fields for they are ready to harvest. Will you work in God's field?

If you merely *repeat* a prayer, it's possible that you will *repeat* a sin. However, if you *repent* of that sin, there is a good chance that you will never *repeat* it again.

Worship is not about showing off and showing out. It's about showing forth the praises of the God who called you out of darkness into His marvelous light.

> 1 Peter 2:9
> But ye are a chosen generation, a royal priesthood, an holy nation, a peculiar people; that ye should show forth the praises of him who hath called you out of darkness into his marvellous light.

It's true that God *looks over* your life, but He will not *over-look* your sin. He wants you to repent.

Our Heavenly Father found a lot of our Founding Fathers. He's ready to find some more of our elected officials.

Shadrach, Meshach, and Abednego were faced with a situation where they had to choose the worldly king or the Heavenly Father. If you know this familiar Bible story, you know what happened. They stood up for their convictions, then God honored them and delivered them from the fiery furnace. As I pondered this passage this morning, something dawned on me. These three guys were not disrespectful in their verbiage TO the king or ABOUT the king. Without calling him rude names, they merely said, "O king, we cannot do what you ask us to do."

They stood for their convictions without destroying their witness of how to talk to an authority figure. I have a hunch that if we, as Christians, would stand up for what we believe without name calling, then people would see that our conversation matches our conversion. I firmly believe if we do that, God will show up in the fire that we are facing one more time.

It's true that God will not give you more than you can handle. But, what if God would not let you handle more than you give?

The Bible says that God is coming back for a glorious church without spot or wrinkle. You get spots from *sinning*, but you get wrinkles from *sitting*. God isn't looking for a sinning or a sitting church. Let's get up and get busy winning souls to Christ.

Just as the moon is a reflection of the sun, serving people is a reflection of serving the Son of God.

In life, you will have trials. You will also make errors.

But God never meant for trial and error to be used together. Your trial wasn't meant for you to make an error; it was meant for God to make and mold you into His image!

> 1 Peter 1:7
> That the trial of your faith, being much more precious than of gold that perisheth, though it be tried with fire, might be found unto praise and honour and glory at the appearing of Jesus Christ:

If a Church is doing its job, people can come as they are but never leave as they were.

Finding the *good* in others will help them find the *God* in you.

What if we stopped accusing people of falling from grace, and instead, be the arms that reach out to help them fall into grace?

The Christian race is not about who runs the farthest, the fastest. It's about finishing to live with the Father.

I'm less than perfect, but I'm more than a conqueror.

Romans 8:37
Nay, in all these things we are more than conquerors through him that loved us.

You will never be good enough.
That's why you serve a God who is more than enough.

Psalm 14:3
They are all gone aside, they are all together become filthy: there is none that does good, no, not one.

It's impossible to be *led* by the Spirit of God without being *fed* by the Word of God!

> Hebrews 5:12
> For when for the time ye ought to be teachers, ye have need that one teach you again which be the first principles of the oracles of God; and are become such as have need of milk, and not of strong meat.

Christianity is more than weekly talk; it is a daily walk.

> James 1:22
> But be ye doers of the word, and not hearers only, deceiving your own selves.

A dress code without a moral code is nothing more than a cover-up.

> Genesis 3:7
> And the eyes of them both were opened, and they knew that they were naked; and they sewed fig leaves together, and made themselves aprons.

Just because you fell on your face while trying doesn't mean that you need to lay there dying. Your failure might have frightened you, but it didn't finish you.

> Micah 7:8
> Rejoice not against me, O mine enemy: when I fall, I shall arise; when I sit in darkness, the Lord shall be a light unto me.

Standing on your tiptoes will not get you a better view of God. Getting on your knees with your eyes closed is a far better way to see Him.

Refuse to be *confined* by the way you are *defined* by people while God is *refining* you.

Jumping to conclusions is the only exercise that some people get.

> Ecclesiastes 12:13
> Let us hear the conclusion of the whole matter: Fear God, and keep his commandments: for this is the

whole duty of man.

Since God does not categorize sin, be careful that your reaction to someone else's action does not make you guilty of a different sin with the same consequences.

1 Peter 4:15
But let none of you suffer as a murderer, or as a thief, or as an evildoer, or as a busybody in other men's matters.

"In God We Trust" is *inscribed* on our money, but it is also *described* in our giving.

Your application for fruit inspector was received, but it has already been filled-by God.

Your job will be to continue to grow fruit and not inspect the fruit of others.

John 15:5, 8
I am the vine, you are the branches: He that abides in me, and I in him, the same brings forth much fruit: for without me ye can do nothing. Herein is my Father glorified, that ye bear much fruit;

so shall ye be my disciples.

Since Christ has an *inner view* of you, when He asks you to come and chat, it is not an *interview*. He already knows your condition and wants to hear you confess it.

> Isaiah 1:18
> Come now, and let us reason together, saith the Lord: though your sins be as scarlet, they shall be as white as snow; though they be red like crimson, they shall be as wool.

To be strong physically, you have to lift weights. To be strong spiritually, you have to lay aside weights.

> Hebrews 12:1
> Wherefore seeing we also are compassed about with so great a cloud of witnesses, let us lay aside every weight, and the sin which doth so easily beset us, and let us run with patience the race that is set before us.

God's answer of *no* might put a damper on your day, but it will definitely put delight in your destiny.

Romans 8:28

And we know that all things work together for good to them that love God, to them who are the called according to his purpose.

We need to take people off of our hit list and put them on our prayer list.

Matthew 5:44

But I say unto you, Love your enemies, bless them that curse you, do good to them that hate you, and pray for them which despitefully use you, and persecute you;

You cannot *alter* your past. You have to *altar* it.

Romans 3:25

Whom God hath set forth to be a propitiation through faith in his blood, to declare his righteousness for the remission of sins that are past, through the forbearance of God.

Running people down is not considered exercise, but lifting them up will strengthen you both.

Galatians 6:1
Brethren, if a man be overtaken in a fault, ye which are spiritual, restore such an one in the spirit of meekness; considering thyself, lest thou also be tempted.

It's impossible to clear your head until you allow God to clean your heart.

Psalm 51:10
Create in me a clean heart, O God; and renew a right spirit within me.

The world says that it's better to be safe than sorry.
Christianity says that being sorry is the only way to be safe.

2 Corinthians 7:10
Godly sorrow brings repentance that leads to salvation and leaves no regret, but worldly sorrow brings death.

One of my favorite verses in the Bible is:

1 Peter 4:15
But let none of you suffer as a murderer, or as a
thief, or as an evildoer, or as a busybody in other
men's matters.

Notice the sins listed: murderer, thief, evildoer, and busybody.

How in the world can these four sins be listed in the same
verse? I think it's because they are equal in the sight of God.

A busybody can do as much damage as a murderer, a thief,
and an evildoer.

I'm so thankful to Pastor a Church where we don't have
busybodies; we have people that keep their bodies busy working
for the Lord!

True Christians are not those who are waiting for
people to fall.

But they are there to catch them and care for them if they do.

Galatians 6:1
Dear brothers and sisters, if another believer is overcome by some sin, you who are godly should gently
and humbly help that person back onto the right
path. And be careful not to fall into the same temptation yourself.

Very few people will *wander* into a church.

That's why Christians have to take the *wonder* into the world.

Acts 6:8
And Stephen, full of faith and power, did great wonders and miracles among the people.

Christianity is more like *setting your sails* than *starting your engines*. It's not how fast you start; it's the consistency it takes to get to the other shore.

Ecclesiastes 9:11
I returned, and saw under the sun, that the race is not to the swift, nor the battle to the strong, neither yet bread to the wise, nor yet riches to men of understanding, nor yet favour to men of skill; but time and chance happeneth to them all.

A church is where people gather.
Evangelism is where you gather people.

Sometimes God fights *for* us. Other times He fights *through* us.

In our Christian faith, what we know and what they know has to be the same.

1 John 3:14
We know that we have passed from death unto life, because we love the brethren. He that loveth not his brother abideth in death.

John 13:35
By this shall all men know that ye are my disciples, if ye have love one to another.

Why is it that people close their eyes when they want to kiss, but they can't close their mouths when they want to cuss?

We eagerly anticipate whatever the next big event is in life. Whether it's the next vacation or something as major as a marriage, we count down the days. But in the big picture of life, there is no event more significant than standing before Jesus.

So, while we are counting down the days for small trips, let's make the days count as we prepare for the journey of our lifetime, the destination that will last for all of eternity.

Sometimes, Jesus is more interested in *sitting with you* than you *setting things up for Him.*

As a Christian, it's our calling to serve the Lord. But everyone who serves needs to find time to sit at the feet of Jesus.

I love my early mornings of sitting at His feet before I start my day of serving Him and others.

> Luke 10: 38-42
> Now it came to pass, as they went, that he entered into a certain village: and a certain woman named Martha received him into her house. And she had a sister called Mary, which also sat at Jesus' feet, and heard his word. But Martha was cumbered about much serving, and came to him, and said, Lord, dost thou not care that my sister hath left me to serve alone? bid her therefore that she help me. And Jesus answered and said unto her, Martha, Martha, thou art careful and troubled about many things: But one thing is needful: and Mary hath chosen that good part, which shall not be taken away from her.

In Matthew 6, in the passage we call "The Lord's Prayer," we read what is really our prayer that the Lord told us to pray.

While it's self-explanatory, there is also the fact of knowing that when you pray this prayer, it requires total surrender.

If you look carefully at verse 10, you read what is written, but you also have clarity into what wasn't written.

It's impossible to have:

THY Kingdom COME without MY Kingdom GO.

THY will be DONE without I'm DONE with MY will.

Matthew 6:9-12

After this manner therefore pray ye: Our Father which art in heaven, Hallowed be thy name. Thy kingdom come. Thy will be done in earth, as it is in heaven. Give us this day our daily bread. And forgive us our debts, as we forgive our debtors. And lead us not into temptation, but deliver us from evil: For thine is the kingdom, and the power, and the glory, for ever. Amen.

God will never allow you to box Him in, but He will let you lock Him out.

Revelation 3:20
Behold, I stand at the door, and knock: if any man hear my voice, and open the door, I will come in to him, and will sup with him, and he with me.

People do not want God to have selective hearing when they pray, but they pray that He has selective seeing when they stray.

Don't allow the past tense of your life to make the present so tense that you miss God's plan for your future tense.

Most people can only keep their ducks in a row for a few days in a row.

People who talk *to* God in private do not mind talking to people *about* God in public.

Don't draw a line in the sand. Build a house upon the Rock.

It does not matter how many lines you draw in the sand. At some point in life, the tide will get high enough to wash your lines away.

Matthew 7:24-27

Therefore whosoever heareth these sayings of mine, and doeth them, I will liken him unto a wise man, which built his house upon a rock: And the rain descended, and the floods came, and the winds blew, and beat upon that house; and it fell not: for it was founded upon a rock. And every one that heareth these sayings of mine, and doeth them not, shall be likened unto a foolish man, which built his house upon the sand: And the rain descended, and the floods came, and the winds blew, and beat upon that house; and it fell: and great was the fall of it.

To be a *peacekeeper*, you have to be a *peacemaker*.

Matthew 5:9
Blessed are the peacemakers: for they shall be called
the children of God.

What you *profess* with your mouth, you must *possess* in
your heart.

Luke 6:45
A good man out of the good treasure of his heart bringeth forth that which is good; and an evil man out
of the evil treasure of his heart bringeth forth that
which is evil: for of the abundance of the heart his
mouth speaketh.

God is not limited by little; He is only limited by what you
won't let Him have.

Everybody wants a new Genesis, but not everyone is willing
to make an Exodus.
Genesis is a beginning, while Exodus is a departure.
Everyone is so anxious for a new start, but very few are willing
to stop their old way of doing things.

The Bible clearly states that God has called us out of darkness (an exodus) into His marvelous light (a new beginning-a Genesis).

Old things are passed away, and all things become new. Every new beginning means there has to be an old ending.

I was excited about my new tricycle until I wanted a bicycle. I was excited about my new bicycle until I wanted a mini-bike. I was excited about my new mini-bike until I wanted a car. I was excited about my new car until I wanted a newer car...You get the gist.

Life has a way of making you outgrow some things...but the truth is, the more we have, the more we want.

My question is, why can't we be that way about God?

I was saved when I was 9. It was a great experience. However, as my age progressed, I wanted to go deeper in Him and know more about Him. Today, as a 59-year-old man, I still want more of Him.

Too many Christians get saved, and there is no progression in their walk with the Lord. They are still riding a tricycle when God wants them to fly.

Getting saved is not just a place to stop sinning; it's a place to start serving. Salvation begins a journey that will take you out of this world. Paul said it best when he said, "From glory to glory."

Don't let getting saved stop you from getting all of the other gifts that God has for you!

Turbulence usually makes everyone use the name of God. Some call on His name for help while others take it in vain.

Repenting of a sin saves you from the repeating of a cycle.

If you *inhale* the breath of eternal Life, you will not be *in hell* for the rest of your life!

> John 20:22
> And when he had said this, he breathed on them, and saith unto them, Receive ye the Holy Ghost:

If turning over a new leaf is not working for you, you might want to consider putting down some new roots.

People that never get to the root of the problem can never branch very far from where they are. The root always affects the branch.

Every moment of life will not go down in History as monumental. For example, Noah only built one Ark, but he built many altars.

When God was ready to destroy man from the face of the earth, He faced a man standing at an altar. And Noah found grace in the eyes of the Lord.

We know Noah as the man that built the Ark, but had he not previously built an altar, he would have never been asked to build an Ark.

Also, the first thing he did when he got off of the Ark was to erect an altar. We identify him by the big thing that he did, but God identified him by the daily thing that he did at the altar.

Every moment of life is not a monumental moment in the eyes of people, but daily discipleship is what makes the big things happen.

In Conclusion

Every head bowed; every eye closed. Just kidding. I know that I am not ending a sermon, but I pray that this book has been an ending to some of your questions and the beginning of new inspiration. Hopefully, one particular quip or quote will become a part of your life and will become a reference point to know that the greatest Author of all time gave one of His little authors a word to help you.

Maybe you have read a quote or two from this book and you are not a Christian. As believers in Christ, we often have our own lingo and catchy Christian phrases. However, most of the content of this book comes from a life of knowing Christ and being around people that are trying their best to become the best version of themselves possible. Being a Christian is truly an honor because of what Jesus did for us on the cross of Calvary.

Interwoven into every interval of this book is a little bit of my life. I have been blessed with so many things to cherish, but I also have faced many challenges. Many of these quotes were written during dark times of my life. Even though discouragement visited me many times, my only choice was to persevere. Jesus was not a light at the end of the tunnel; He was my life in the middle of my trouble. When I could not coin a phrase, I could always come up with a praise, and I thank God for being a Man of His Word.

If you do not know Him in that way, I would love for you to contact me and quiz me about this "Quistian" life. Who knows, in my next book there may be a whole page devoted to you, as you inspire me to write another quip, quote, or question for you as a new Quistian!

About the Author

Tommy and Ann Galloway are the Senior Pastors at Word of Life Church in Tupelo, Mississippi. When the Church was founded in 1996, Pastor Tommy coined the phrase: "Leading locally, reaching regionally, and growing globally." Over the past 23 years, those words have certainly been fulfilled. People drive from several counties to WOLC every Sunday. Pastor Tommy speaks weekly on the **Words of Life Broadcast** on NBC, while Ann and he travel regionally and globally to share *Quips, Quotes, and Questions to Quistians (Christians)* on different parts of the globe.

CPSIA information can be obtained
at www.ICGtesting.com
Printed in the USA
LVHW021905030220
645693LV00019B/1236